Donald

with affection

Andy

2 March 1987

FICTIONAL DISCOURSE AND HISTORICAL SPACE

FICTIONAL DISCOURSE AND HISTORICAL SPACE

Andrew Wright
Professor of English
University of California
San Diego

MACMILLAN
PRESS

First published 1987
Published by
THE MACMILLAN PRESS LTD
Houndsmills, Basingstoke, Hampshire RG21 2XS
and London
Companies and representatives
throughout the world

Printed in Hong Kong

British Library Cataloguing in Publication Data
Wright, Andrew, 1923 –
Fictional discourse and historical space.
1. English fiction — History and
criticism
I. Title
823'.009   PR821
ISBN 0–333–40805–5

For
Daphne, Peter, Evangeline, and Tenniel

Contents

Note

Several sentences of the introduction have been borrowed from a lecture, 'The Novel as a Conspiracy', published in *Essays by Divers Hands: Being the Transactions of the Royal Society of Literature*, n.s. 37 (1972), 122–33.

1 Introduction

While reading *The Mosquito Coast*, that frightening but ultimately hopeful Crusoe novel of the 1980s, I thought back to Defoe's great original of 1719; and, when I re-read that novel, I learned from the juxtaposition something more about the work of both Defoe and Theroux. From that point other contiguities suggested themselves. The outcome is the present study: there are three pairs of novels, each pair treating a similar subject, and each member of the pair being removed in time from the other – 263 years divide Defoe's novel from that of Theroux; nearly a century *Emma* from *Howards End*, and three quarters of a century *The Secret Agent* from *The Human Factor*.

Common sense raises a preliminary objection to this way of proceeding, and common sense also meets the objection, which is that there are hazards in making such comparisons: each of the six writers under scrutiny is unique. Granted; but each work in speaking for itself speaks also for its age in that each embodies more fully its age's possibilities, and each sketches the lineaments of that age, the more so in that each is generally representative and on the highest level. To choose six other great writers and six other novels would be to make necessary a different series of findings, a different picture from what appears in these pages. Yes, a somewhat different picture, but not one altogether different, unless one were to select works of the second rank. For I do claim importance for my writers and their texts – by which I mean that they are of such stature as to embody claims to comprehensiveness, though not of course exhaustiveness. Obviously, there is more than one way to write a history, and there are other important novelists than the six I have chosen; if instead of Defoe and Theroux, Jane Austen and Forster, Conrad and Graham Greene, I had selected Richardson and Virginia Woolf, Walter Scott and Hardy, Dickens and Naipaul, this would have been a different book, but it would bear recognizable resemblances to what the reader has before him. Nor do I think exhaustive treatment is either desirable or necessary; the aim here is exemplary and explanatory rather than encompassing.

Mainly, the aim here is practical, to elucidate the novels under consideration. My highest hope is that the readers of this book will regard the interpretations offered in the following pages as helpful. If they are so, part at least of the cause will be because of a sense of new discovery that stems from a reading of a number of literary and historical critics of the present day, especially Michel Foucault, Fredric Jameson, and Hayden White, all of whom have taught me much about history, about narrative, and about the place of literature in thought. Others too have taken me back to school: Robert Alter, Robert Caserio, Jacques Derrida, Suzanne Gearhart, Gérard Genette, Frank Kermode, Murray Krieger, Frank Lentricchia, David Lodge, Walter J. Ong, Roy Pascal, Shlomith Rimmon-Kenan, Walter Slatoff, Tzvetan Todorov, Harold Toliver, and Marianna Torgovnick. If I have failed to include on this list the names of Wayne C. Booth and Ian Watt, the reason is that they are so much a part of the critical air we breathe, so indispensable to all readers at every point, that they belong in a separate category. And Watt's work on Conrad will find special application here. My indebtedness to the others will emerge in the following pages. But I want to begin by sketching my way of proceeding.

The writing of history is a literary enterprise, as Gibbon himself indicated; by the same token, all literature belongs to history – a claim, or truism even, that would not need to be repeated except for the fact that it has been intermittently contested or ignored in literary criticism for the last forty years, to the considerable detriment of our understanding. The divorce between the writing of history and the writing that is avowedly fictional cannot take place because the two are not separate imaginative endeavours but a single entity, despite the efforts of the New Criticism of the 1940s and 1950s, which I was brought up on. Such confusion as exists stems from another, and actual, difference, that between events that have indisputably or supposedly happened and the accounts of those events that constitute what is called history, the former being the materials out of which the historian makes his constructions, which are the literary product of the historian's practice of his art. As historical writing is a rationalization after the event, historians make plots out of what they think has really happened, imposing a pattern on what they have discerned by selecting certain events out of the undifferentiated mass of facts and suppositions, and arranging them in a certain order. Those who compose avowedly fictional narratives are – deceptively – somewhat more free, but they too take the materials that observation furnishes, and try to make sense of them by arranging them into discourses. All men of letters are, as Hayden White has insisted, moralists. There is, in Suzanne Gearhart's elegant phrase, an open boundary between history and fiction. At the same time I agree with Harold Toliver that history and fiction, though similar, are not identical: 'consequential logic teases out its revelations with more design and foresight in the novelist than it does in Gibbon and Hume' (15). Likewise, the demand in both history and fiction for signifying shape and ultimately closure is, Hayden White argues, 'a demand . . . for moral meaning, a demand that the sequences of . . . events be assessed as to their significance as elements of a *moral* drama. . . . Where, in any account of reality, narrativity is present we can be sure that morality or a moralizing impulse is present too' (White 1981, 20–22).

The idea behind the idea of history is that the past can be recaptured, but it is sometimes assumed that assiduity combined with common sense will somehow open the way to such recovery; yet it is common sense after all that reveals another substructure of supposition, namely that all who go to the past do so with the tools of their hypotheses; like other members of the human race who are interested in looking backwards, historians go to the past either in the hope of hope or on some other premise, for instance the premise that the more it changes the more it remains the same. The outcome of the investigations, in other words, will show the way forward in such a way as to make possible the avoidance of the mistakes of the past; or, on the contrary, such investigation will confirm the preliminary fear that there is no way forward, that mankind will keep repeating forever its original and tragic errors.

There is a way of side-stepping both the pleasures of hope and the pains of despair, and that is to refuse to be interested at all in the subject of history. It is not only Henry Ford who thought history to be bunk; his is a thoroughly American statement of the case, with roots in American civilization itself, and with intellectually respectable exemplars, including Emerson and William James. Henry Ford's dictum brings to mind the Corporal in Derek Walcott's play, *Dream on Monkey Mountain:* he says 'History . . . is just one series of breach of promise' (261–62). And in *The Return of Eva Perón,* V.S. Naipaul writes: 'There is no history in Argentina. There are no archives; there are only graffiti and polemics and school lessons' (113). And it is more than plausible to suppose that some at least of the present-day avoidance of historical study springs from the fear of what might be found. This undertaking is not for them, but for those who acknowledge that literary study is also historical study of a particularly promising kind. It is for those who recognize that the practice of history is the practice of story-telling, of putting the past into narrative form, an enterprise that requires not only an idea of meaning but also the exercise of an art. It is, as Foucault argues, an act of power.

By 'historical space' in the title I mean to propose no new and exclusive way of looking at history. It is true, however, that Foucault has made everyone think again about what history is – as a subject, as a discipline, as an art; and while he has attracted a certain amount of controversy in the setting forth of his views, he has convinced many people, including me. There is succession, time passes, the ideas of one generation give way to those of another; we are constrained; it is different to be alive now from what it was to be alive in 1719. Moreover, I accept Hayden White's argument that any construction of historical narrative is: construction of narrative, a series of choices that introduces fictiveness into any historical effort. So far am I willing to see the notion of history reconsidered; and I think it is of the first importance that it should be reconsidered. But I am not embarked on the troubled, though sometimes exhilarating, waters of literary theory as such. Let me just say that I am indeed exhilarated by Fredric Jameson's assertion that narrative is 'the central function or *instance* of the human mind' (13) – these are truly inspiring words, for to join the terms of history and narrative is an undertaking well worth while on account of the illumination that the junction provides; and when Jameson goes on to say that narrative is 'a symbolic resolution to a concrete historical situation' (117), I am the more hopeful of a result that will be useful here.

So the point of departure of the present study is the observation – at once obvious, irresistible, and urgent – that no novel can escape its historical moment: *Robinson Crusoe* belongs to the second decade of the eighteenth century and to an England restless in its parliamentary triumph over the divine right of kings as it is triumphant also in its protestant – its dissenting – particularity. To repeat Defoe's effort, as many have done, is to pay a compliment that itself has a respectable history, from the feeble contemporary imitations of Defoe to *The Swiss Family Robinson* and Michel Tournier's *Friday*; but as every historical moment is different from every other, having unique prefigurative aspects and at the same time fluid contexts as well as different sequential possibilities, *The*

Mosquito Coast, like all other Crusoe novels, must stand as a separate achievement because it belongs to a different moment, a different culture, a different nation.

Yet discreteness is not all; the second decade of the eighteenth century is not unrecognizable in the 1980s. The England, at least of 1719 and the New England of Theroux's present-day, display continuities that can be traced, and that must be traced. By the same token the culture of the country gentry represented in Jane Austen reveals profound differences and surprising resemblances to the urban bourgeois high culture that Forster celebrates in *Howards End*. And the sharply-delineated imagination of disaster that Conrad formulated in *The Secret Agent* finds its analogue as well in its apocalyptic development in *The Human Factor*.

Novels, after all, are narratives conscious of their narrativity. They are constructions of the worlds that their authors imagine, based on what they discern, necessitating many kinds of selection, omission, emphasis, rearrangement; and examination of the public and private dimensions of these narratives should reveal a picture of the time in which each has been brought into being. No doubt it is possible to make a self-contained analysis of any novel, self-contained in the sense of requiring the very minimum of what is misleadingly called 'background' knowledge – who Alexander Selkirk was, how Defoe thought and acted in response to the issues of his day, what literary models were available to him; such facts are simply the precondition of understanding. Also, *Robinson Crusoe* is one of those books that has made its appeal to many generations of readers. What it meant to Defoe's intended audience in the second and third decades of the eighteenth century cannot be less important than what it meant to Marx for instance, who read the book idiosyncratically. It is equally true that *The Secret Agent* contains in its final emphasis on the professor who would blow up the world an irony that could not have been intended by Conrad, who knew nothing of the development that was to take place in Los Alamos – and Hiroshima and Nagasaki. So my point here is that the historical space within which a novel is composed sets limits of intended meaning that the work is to have for its immediate readership, and ever afterwards as well; and that as for certain works making repeated claims on the attention of generations of readers – these further interpretations and readings have to be taken into account by those of us who are now experiencing these works in the latter part of the twentieth century.

There is no narration without a narrator. Even the most dramatic of narratives must be *told*, and in the telling is the implication of a manager of the narrative, even when the narrator is shy of showing himself. The claim, as most of my readers will recognize at once, is far from new; Wayne Booth made it the cornerstone of his landmark study of fiction twenty-five years ago, and even then it was (as he knew, and said) not an original discovery. But it is the fact that there appear from time to time assertions – still, in the 1980s – that there is such a phenomenon as the narratorless narrative, and while I do not want to argue against that persistent belief here, I want to take note of it, simply to urge that it be put aside. As David Lodge said only recently: 'In pursuing mimetic methods to their limits, Modernist fiction discovered that you cannot abolish the author, you can only suppress or displace him' (105). Henry James said it plainly, if grandly, almost a hundred years ago: 'The spreading field, the human scene, is the "choice of subject"; the pierced aperture, either broad or balconied or slit-like and low-browed, is the "literary form"; but they are, singly or together, as nothing without the posted presence of the watcher – without, in other words, the consciousness of the artist' (xi). In three words – and they are the authoritative words of Gérard Genette – 'Mimesis is diegesis' (5).

For always the novel has been a conspiracy, sometimes a much disguised conspiracy, between writer and reader. The sense of complicity in this relationship is so deep as to be nearly always surreptitious, the third party being in most cases the hero, the central figure who is (and the reader never fails to know it) uninformed of the most capital and decisive and fateful facts. It is of course the very heart of all narrative strategy, in or out of the novel, that the hero remain ignorant longer than is good for him, but the novel stands apart from all other literary forms in the peculiarly intimate and even private sense in which the reader comes to know the relationships that the plot unfolds. Dramatic irony, which is the quintessence of theatrical effect, works less openly in the novel, but it works wonders there too. In every novel there are at least two plots; at the forefront is the arrangement of the events of the story in such a way as to indicate their significance. Such is plot in the ordinary sense of the word. Then there is a plot also in another sense, in the sense of a private treaty between narrator and reader. In other words, any novel needs not only a narrative – it needs some one to tell it, and the telling transposes it. As Rimmon-Kenan says so trenchantly: 'Narration is always at a higher narrative level than the story it relates' (92). The narrator is someone to be reckoned with.

There has never been a time when narrative strategies were unnecessary. To be sure, a certain amount of nonsense has been written about the ease subsisting between writers and readers in classical ages when communication was easy and assured because founded on shared assumptions. But scrutiny of – for instance – the English eighteenth century, while it does indeed reveal the sense of community celebrated by Addison, by Pope, by Dr Johnson, and by many others of smaller consequence (and evidently taken for granted by most educated men): such scrutiny nevertheless shows that between writer and reader the relationship is always carefully weighed, formulated, arranged. Between writer and reader is never the suspense of strategy; true ease in writing comes from art, not chance. In any event, as Slatoff so sensibly points out: 'Our very decision that a group of works are worth attending to is in part a decision that the teller is worth listening to' (92).

The relationship between narrator and audience *is* doubtless crucially dependent on shared assumptions, which – when the novel to be read is older than yesterday – requires cultural continuity; no work of fiction (or any other work of art) is for a moment self-dependent. Ian Watt has shown that the greatest writers of the neo-classical period employed highly sophisticated devices for sophisticated purposes in this regard – that Fielding, for example, catered to a double audience, the classically educated, and the others (22). This is to say that, even perhaps especially in the most classical of times, and even when the distance between author and narrator has been a narrow one, narrative management is necessary.

Thus in *Tom Jones* Fielding's second self, in the character of the narrator, constructs a hypothetical double audience out of his own experience of life, but it is a pair of audiences that have something in common. To both he appeals, sometimes over the head of one of them, to a universal sense of truths, a *sensus communis* indeed – a compound of good sense, fraternal regard, male delicacy, feminine strength, together with a social order that will contain the best and restrain the worst of human nature. But to what degree is fictiveness involved in the assumptions of the existence of the audience? In an influential essay, called 'The Writer's Audience is Always a Fiction', Walter J. Ong has gone a long way toward making us understand our relationship as readers to any novel.

> The audience must . . . fictionalize itself. A reader has to play
> the role in which the author has cast him, which seldom
> coincides with his role in the rest of actual life. An office worker
> on a bus reading a novel of Thomas Hardy is listening to a voice
> which is not that of any real person in the real setting around
> him. He is playing the role demanded of him by this person
> speaking in quite a special way from the book. . . . Readers over
> the ages have had to learn this game of literacy, how to conform
> themselves to the projections of the writers they read, or at least
> to operate in terms of these projections. They have had to know
> how to play the game of being a member of an audience that
> 'really' does not exist. (12)

Fictional characters must be regarded also as – fictional. For
better rather than worse, they are enclosed within a story that is
recognizable as such. Ordinary characters are aware only intermittently of playing roles in a drama, for the good reason that for
most of the time we are not playing such roles. We may say all the
world's a stage no more frequently than do fictional characters, and
on the whole we know better than to think our lives dramatic. On
the other hand, however forgetful or oblivious fictional characters
may be, we know that they are the creatures of the plots their
creators construct. Fictional characters *do* something, and what
they do counts in the sense that issues are raised and ultimately
resolved; they are forced to perform, by a narrator. For every
fictional Tess enchanted until she is no longer intact there are
countless young women seduced by men who charm them – but
there is a difference: if there were not we should say that they
belong to a world of fiction rather than of life. Tess at Stonehenge is
magnificent; outside the novel the episode would be mere melodrama. *Our* lives, forever the prey of luck and accident, have shape
only retrospectively if at all. As Barbara Leah Harman says, 'A man
purchases an image of coherent life at the expense of his knowledge
that life is an ongoing, and sometimes a chaotic, affair' (865). To
know oneself is to make a fiction of one's life, to contain it within a
narrative that is by definition sequential, that begins and ends in
the past. The reader's judgement of fictions is therefore two-
dimensional: the first assesses the character in so far as his actions
can be understood objectively so to speak; the second assesses the

narrator's character as witness. In fiction we are at the mercy of a third party. The only fictional evidence is hearsay.

There is also the idiom of fictional narration. 'Idiom' is a convenient word, perhaps too convenient, in that it may offer shelter behind which to hide one's awe at the mystery of particularity. Identification of idiom in this sense is one of the tasks of criticism, and yet to stop with such apprehension is to stop short. It does not matter at all, except perhaps when passing examinations, that a given passage is by Jane Austen or George Eliot or Virginia Woolf, unless this knowledge provides some further access. The important question is not what makes the idiom, but what the idiom intends to convey, and convey within the work. The novel, not the author, or the idiosyncracy, is what matters. And the key to the language of fiction is the idiom of the story teller. To understand the narrator's turns of phrase in exactly the senses called for is the essence of knowing what to make of a novel. All the more important, therefore, to realize that the narrator may seem to compass more or less than, or something different from, what he appears to intend.

All six of the novels in the present study must be accounted realistic, and when the term is used – or the phenomenon observed – the question of reality is inevitably raised. For realism is a convention, and reality is – something else. In a magisterial essay of wide influence Marshall Brown has shown (not for the first time) that reality is not actuality itself but a construction of the mind: 'Reality', he says 'is . . . not a given or an absolute, to be found in all matter at all times: it is a particular structure of relationships, one among many different manifestations of being. It is incorrect to say that reality simply "exists" and that realistic writing imitates it; rather reality is one possible ordering of things, just as realism is one possible ordering of texts' (234). Accordingly realism must be understood not as the strategy of depicting the real but of half-deluding the reader into a sense of actuality; to go further than half way is a mistake. Total delusion is what Partridge suffers at the notable performance of *Hamlet* in *Tom Jones*. For realism is a window, a more or less opaque and more or less elaborately framed window, authenticating (to use Morton Bloomfield's fine word) what is to be viewed and at the same time calling attention to itself as limiting and at the same time transfiguring the scene revealed. Käte Hamburger puts it another way, but just as decisively. 'Whereas a real reality is because it is, a fictive reality "is" only by virtue of its being narrated. . . . The persons in a novel are narrated persons, just as the figures of a painting are painted figures' (136).

Robinson Crusoe is a tale of survival in the wilderness, told many years later by the hero of the adventure, who wants (as he says) to inculcate certain lessons to be derived not only from his original decision to undertake the series of adventures but also from the experience itself. *The Mosquito Coast* is also a tale of survival, or rather of intended and attempted survival, in the wilderness. Here the Crusoe figure is not the narrator of his own story but the subject of the story as related by his adolescent son. In the course of the novel the learning that takes place centres on the son rather than on the father. The connection between the two novels is obvious enough, and there are in fact a number of direct references in *The Mosquito Coast* to *Robinson Crusoe*. By changing the vantage point from which the narrative is presented, Paul Theroux changes, and quite plainly changes by intention, the meaning of his novel; the Crusoe theme is used for a different purpose altogether from that which engaged Defoe's attention. And here is where a danger creeps in. The fairest way to make such a comparison as the one I am undertaking would be in fact impossible; it would be best if Defoe could be exhumed and set to work writing *Robinson Crusoe* in our own day. Defoe was a particular Englishman, with a literary background in sharp contrast to that of Theroux, an American born in Massachusetts. Defoe was a rooted Englishman; Theroux, though he has lived in London for a number of years, remains – as he insists – an American writer. Still, it is my hope that for all the differences that are necessarily exhibited in the production of works by these two different writers, there is some considerable value in the juxtaposition that I have undertaken. The proof of the pudding lies in the pages that follow this introduction.

Of the second pair of novels, *Emma* and *Howards End*, the fact that the first was written by a woman and the second by a man is no doubt capital, but it is a matter that cannot convincingly be worried at, if only because of the inevitable reticences and darknesses of private life. But the similarities in character, together with the sense of gender-determined limitedness of the heroines, can be chronicled. Emma Woodhouse is, her author tells us at the outset, handsome, clever, and rich; in two respects like the heroine of *Howards End:* Margaret Schlegel is certainly clever and rich. The two women are also independent in important senses, Emma in that she is the central figure in her household, 'poor Miss Taylor' having married and left Emma alone and dominant, with her father to look after to be sure; but his authority is perfectly subservient to hers. Margaret Schlegel is independent of parental authority, her parents being dead. She is free too, in that her relationships to her grown-up sister Helen and her almost-grown-up brother Tibby leave her plenty of scope for the exercise of her own will. It is true that Emma Woodhouse is constrained not merely by the peevishness of her father but also by the spoken and unspoken prohibitions of the small society of which she is a part. *Emma* was written at the end of a long period of revolutionary hope and disillusionment and consequent wars, settled only as recently as the year before *Emma* was published. *Howards End* was written toward the end of the hundred-year peace that was made possible by that most unpromising of treaties, the Treaty of Vienna. Unquestionably there was a certain sense of doom at the end of the Edwardian period, such that the note of hope on which *Howards End* concludes is more than a little faint. Forster himself felt in 1908, as his letters reveal, this sense of doom.

The Secret Agent and *The Human Factor* are connected explicitly by the epigraph to the Greene novel, which indeed furnishes the title itself. 'I only know that he who forms a tie is lost. The germ of corruption has entered into his soul.' The Polish *émigré* and the son of the Berkhamsted schoolmaster have more in common than the themes of these two books; they are driven, very restlessly, to try to make sense of life in worlds different in some respects, but similar also in others. Greene's world is an exacerbation of that which Conrad foresaw.

Connections between these six novels can also be made in other ways, and they are interesting enough to contemplate. Theroux admires Graham Greene and has demonstrated this regard in *Picture Palace,* which contains a splendid and also affectionate portrait of Greene. Forster regarded Jane Austen highly and went to school to her for some aspects of his style. Greene has repeatedly acknowledged a sense of indebtedness to Conrad. But to pursue these connections and a number of others as well would be to complicate, even perhaps obscure, what I am up to. For what I should like to be able to do in the following pages is no more and no less than to provide a series of fresh and useful readings. By virtue of bearing witness to the times in which they were produced, the novels of which I am writing demonstrate something about those times.

There is an underlying assumption in what follows, namely that coherence is indispensable for the production of a work of literary art, and coherence is a test of the work's success. Yet to me one of the reasons for the immense attractiveness of Derrida is his discovery in discourse itself of the element of the indeterminate, on account of the limitations of language and also on account of the differences in human response that make for variation in the experiencing of a literary work. This is the element now called undecidability, which exists in even the most coherent of literary structures. Partial truths are all we can expect, and if we try to mine the novelists for more than these, we shall be not only disappointed but worse: we shall be asking for what they cannot give and ought not to be expected to give, a grand vision of the unseen, the unseeable, the unenvisionable. Nonetheless, the victory of coherence over chaos is a victory for civilization itself.

2   Crusoe Then and Now

I   *ROBINSON CRUSOE:* OR, DO IT YOURSELF

Robinson Crusoe is about living alone and liking it – about preferring solitude to society. It is about turning one's back on one's fellow man because self-sufficiency is the largest and most satisfying sort of fulfillment. There is an inference to be drawn from its instant and continuing success; the book was, and is, timely. Why the celebration of solitude should command such wide attention is, in part at least, an historical question, and within the framework of the answer lies the possibility of understanding more fully both the age and its greatest novel. To begin with Defoe himself: he was, notoriously, an opportunist – thank goodness, for opportunism is the essence of art; but like every other writer Defoe knew that he must take his fair hour in the light of the absolute necessity to be understood by the readers whom he knew he must woo and win if his art was to succeed. The readily available models on which he built were the spiritual autobiography and the castaway account; and these he blended with rare force and unique success. George Starr and J. Paul Hunter have already demonstrated at length the importance of the fact that Defoe had ready to hand the structure of an improving relation based on the crucial fact of conversion (Starr, chapter three; Hunter, chapter six). Nor do the real-life models provided by the accounts of Alexander Selkirk's sojourn to Juan Fernandez, Robert Knox's to Ceylon, and Robert Drury's to Madagascar exhaust the possibilities of accounts on which Defoe could conveniently draw. There is also a specifically biographical framework within which Defoe constructed his fable, as Geoffrey M. Sill has demonstrated (148–71). Seizing his opportunities, Defoe chose to narrate the story of *Robinson Crusoe* in the first person, as if written by its central figure and hero, as a spiritual autobiography that has struck few readers as going more than skin deep; and he made of the castaway story something far more profound than has ever been fashioned since – representing, in the process, the tension in the England of the first two decades of the eighteenth century, so tightly drawn in its conformities, with the threat of dissociation, rejection, exile, if the price were not paid, that is if the exact amount were not forthcoming on demand.

Of course, *Robinson Crusoe* is also a fable of modern man, for from the eighteenth century at least, man has been modern in the sense of being more or less the victim of the state systems that ask so much and return so little, which threaten to swallow individuality in communal imperative. But Defoe's hero succeeds where all the rest of us fail: he achieves selfhood, fulfilment, completeness – by making himself into a one-man society, by forsaking all others, the success being in signal proportion to the dimness with which he recognizes the misanthropic centre of what he takes to be his everlasting soul. That is to say, he pays a price for his success, more of a price than any of his readers could be expected to pay; the fact that all the rest of us can entertain the dream of Robinson Crusoe says something about our secret selves. In bringing to light the side of man that rejects anarchically all society, which eschews the human race altogether, which admits indifference at best or hatred rather than love of one's fellow man: by doing these things Defoe has evidently struck a chord that has sounded and resounded generation after generation since 1719. If, as Hayden White says (1981), narratives are in effect the structures of desire built in the light of public possibility, that is to say within the limits of the power of the state, and as such power may be granted to individuals; if, moreover, as White also says in the same place, plots necessarily *moralize*, then the plot of *Robinson Crusoe* puts together a programme for behaviour, for heroism even, in a society in which the middle state of the middle classes can be escaped and embraced at one and the same time. Robinson Crusoe has his bourgeois cake and eats it too; and that is just the point; but the cost is enormous – it is everything, it is death; and to that theme I shall come, as Crusoe himself comes to it, before the end. For it is an historical theme, springing from the circumstances of the modernity of Defoe's time, and among other things *Robinson Crusoe* demonstrates the continuity of western civilization since the beginning of the eighteenth century. The morbid bourgeois daydream is still with us.

To begin with the form in which the novel is cast, that of the autobiography, it should be observed at once that the laws of autobiography are shifty, depending on the quality of self-esteem of the subject. But whether there is to be a complacent recital of triumphs or an outraged record of failures – or something in between – all autobiography is necessarily self-justificatory, egocentric, vaunting. The autobiographer sets himself above the crowd even when – and especially when – he claims that he is a nobody, or no different from any one else. All autobiographers walk a tightrope, blandly seeming to claim that all men with two legs can walk suspended above the crowd, yet at the same time demonstrating extraordinary powers of balance and force of character. Fictional autobiography belongs within the scope of these remarks no less than factual autobiography, for every auto-biography is a work of art, whether it claims to be true to life or not; it is a rearrangement and so is bound to omit and emphasize in ways that life itself does not; retrospect grants insights that were not available when the events being recounted took place.[1] As Jean Starobinski says: 'The past can never be evoked except with respect to a present: the "reality" of by-gone days is only such to the consciousness which, today, gathering up their present image, cannot avoid imposing upon them its own form, its style' (74). Likewise Roy Pascal points out that 'Autobiography is . . . an interplay, a collusion, between past and present: its significance is indeed more the revelation of the present situation than the un-covering of the past' (11). Obviously, it is correct to think of an autobiographer as one who writes in the present and for the present. And there is an historical basis for the development of the genre. Roy Pascal shows that autobiography is 'a distinctive pro-duct of Western, post-Roman civilisation, and only in modern times has it spread to other civilisations. It postulates a preoccupation with the self that may and often does, deteriorate into vanity, complacency, self-indulgence. But in its best examples, of which there are many, it holds the balance between the self and the world, the subjective and the objective' (180).

In other words, autobiography itself has a past; it is rooted in the individualism that became possible at the beginning of the eighteenth century, against the grain of and in part a reaction to the intensified organisation of the communal state. Also, any narrative necessarily involves development: all novels, for instance, whether autobiographical or not, are Bildungsromanen, records of the education of their heroes or heroines. Robinson Crusoe is supposed to be different at the end of his narrative than he was at the beginning; he is writing a cautionary tale, the ostensible purpose of which is to inculcate the lesson of filial obedience. But, as is manifest from the beginning, the real lesson of the account is exactly the opposite of the didacticism of the prosy old man who is the hero of the novel. And it is the disparity between the

---

[1] Olney (1980) surveys the ground usefully. See his introduction.

announced and actual motive that enables us at once to draw a line between Crusoe and Defoe, and to distance ourselves from the lesson-drawings of its hero. *Robinson Crusoe* contains a lesson all right, but the moral is that of evasion, even unto death.[2]

The presence of an editor – fictional, of course, in fictional autobiographies – makes for a dimension that cannot be neglected, the convention of a scholar who gathers and perhaps arranges the papers of the subject of the autobiography, with a pious and edifying purpose. The editor of *Robinson Crusoe* no less than the editors of *Gulliver's Travels* and *Pamela* and *The Sorrows of Young Werther* commands attention both as moral preceptor, and – covertly – as the sophisticated intermediary between the more or less naive hero and the more or less worldly reader.

However, because *Robinson Crusoe* has so often been read as half-extrapolated autobiography or as a pure adventure story, these remarks may be worth underscoring. It is not irrelevant to trace in Defoe's own outer experience analogues to the journey taken by Crusoe, and this very investigation has been undertaken by the most erudite Defoe scholar now active, Maximillian Novak himself, and his conjectures are compelling (Novak 1983): they must always be considered here, though bafflements remain. These, however, are not central to our own response to the work of imagination that Defoe produced; surely its popularity, from the moment of its publication in 1719 to the present day, depends not on its fidelity to the facts of Defoe's own life, but on its representation and of course transfiguration of certain psychic actualities in a social context. There is something clandestine, even attractively furtive, about *Robinson Crusoe*, and I should say that the revelation of our secret selves set out there is somewhat hideously reassuring. Crusoe has solved the problem of life's complexity by eliminating everything irrelevant to self-possession, including (we are startled to find) sex. What remains is a simplified, thoroughly childish world in which Robinson Crusoe is splendidly successful; here is a regressive dream of such potency that the novel must take its place as one of the most compelling of all literary works.

The Preface to *Robinson Crusoe*, only four short paragraphs long,

---

[2] Michael Boardman has sought to solve the problem of the narrative anomalies in the novel by proposing that there are three narrative stances, the reportorial, the personally detached, and the personally involved; and this is in some ways an attractive solution, but the cost is that of acquiescing in the notion of *Robinson Crusoe* as a miscellany. It seems to me that the lasting impact of the book is unitary rather than tripartite – Boardman 29 et passim.

is modest both in its scope and in its claims. It is also entirely conventional in its assertions that the story is interesting, edifying, and true. But the attitudinizing is important here ('The Editor believes the thing to be a just History of Fact, neither is there any Appearance of fiction in it' [1], setting the terms for the detachment, a patronizing attitude that is implicit throughout the narrative, making for some – though not perhaps a great deal – of the force of the whole. I have already said that every novel is a conspiracy between writer and reader. So it is with *Robinson Crusoe*. A single example may serve to make this point. When Crusoe is endeavouring to explain to Friday the relationship between God and the devil, Friday makes the capital objection: *'If God much strong, much might as the Devil, why God no kill the Devil, so make him no more do wicked?'* Crusoe records his response as follows:

> I was strangely surpriz'd at his Question, and after all, tho' I was now an old Man, yet I was but a young Doctor, and ill enough quallified for a Casuist, or a Solver of Difficulties; and at first I could not tell what to say, so I pretended not to hear him, and ask'd him what he said? But he was too earnest for an Answer to forget his Question; so that he repeated it in the very same broken Words, as above. By this time I had recovered my self a little, and I said, *'God will at last punish him severely; he is reserv'd for the Judgment, and is to be cast into the Bottomless-Pit, to dwell with everlasting fire.'* This did not satisfie *Friday*, but he returns upon me repeating my Words, *'Reserve, at last, me no understand; but, why not kill the Devil now, not kill great ago?'* You may as well ask me, *said I,* 'Why God does not kill you and I, when we do wicked Things here that offend him? We are preserv'd to repent and be pardon'd:' He muses a while at this. *'Well, well,'* says he, mighty affectionately, *'that well; so you, I, Devil, all wicked, all preserve, repent, God pardon all.'* Here I was run down again by him to the last Degree, and it was a Testimony to me, how the meer Notions of Nature, though they will guide reasonable Creatures to the Knowledge of a God, and of a Worship or Homage due to the supreme Being, of God as the Consequence of our Nature; yet nothing but divine Revelation can form the Knowledge of *Jesus Christ* . . .

– and so forth (218–19); and therefore, as he says, he sent Friday off on an errand.[3]

---

[3]Alternatively, as Stephen Prickett has suggested to me, Robinson Crusoe may

There is irony here, not that spacious and contemptuous irony that is so readily observable in Swift and other masters of that sophisticated instrument, but there is the distance making for a judgement on Crusoe that he is unable to discover or perhaps to acknowledge in himself. As a theologian, as in other matters, Crusoe is, to say the least of it, *naive* – or, if you prefer, freshly responsive – and is shown to be so by the deployment of his reflections, musings, arguments, by his blowing hot and cold as danger advances and recedes. But it would be a mistake to re-constitute the novel as a work of labyrinthine and subtle motive, as in their desperation to account for its success a number of critics have tried to do. For *Robinson Crusoe* makes a raw, even a crude, appeal to some of our most elemental instincts, and this appeal is repeatedly exhibited in the multitudinous signs of approbation by the author of his hero. Crusoe is presented as a man to admire, but not for the reasons urged by himself.

The very shape, such as it is, of this novel is worth reflecting on. Gérard Genette (33 ff.) rightly makes a good deal of the temporal duality of Proust's novel; and it is a subject worth remarking in any narrative whatever: in *Robinson Crusoe* the disparity blatantly focuses the reader's attention on what commands the attention of Robinson Crusoe himself. The novel is unbroken by chapter divisions, covering more than six decades of the life of the hero, often with breathless rapidity ('I cannot say that after this, for five Years, any extraordinary thing happened to me, but I liv'd on in the same Course' [136]). The very discontinuousness or strongly episodic quality of the narrative, the weak sense of causality: these are structural principles observable retrospectively and more than anything else indicate that *Robinson Crusoe* is profoundly regressive in its undifferentiating recital of events, episodes, thoughts, opinions: the very featurelessness of the narrative is deeply childish. Mainly, the vantage point is that of an old man now in his

provide this anecdote to show that he was at this point inexperienced in theological argumentation; Friday's question shows that Crusoe is more ignorant than he thought he was. This account exhibits, therefore, not a gap between Defoe and Crusoe but a stage in Crusoe's growing religious awareness. My own feeling is that Robinson would have been explicit in the indication of this development, if he had intended – and if Defoe had intended – what Professor Prickett proposes. Still, it is an argument that must be considered by anyone wishing to make sense of this passage. Pierre Macheray argues that Friday's question about good and evil 'entirely overthrows the distinction' between them (243). On the contrary, the question reveals Crusoe's naiveté about the matter.

seventh decade, looking backward on his youth and on the twenty-eight years he spent on the island at the mouth of the Orinoco River. Repeatedly he reminds his readers that the narrative must be understood in this retrospect, but while he may believe that ripeness is all, his readers (by an inference that Defoe by this strategy forces them to draw) are permitted to understand the pieties in the light of the annuation or superannuation of their declarer. I am not saying that the moral-drawing is altogether subverted by this method, but that it must be taken with a grain or more of salt; it must be understood idiomatically so to speak, rather than straightforwardly.

When Crusoe's father has reminded him of his 'middle state' and urged him to cleave to that state as offering the best opportunity for human happiness, Crusoe says, after the passage of half a century: 'I observed in this last Part of his Discourse, which was truly Prophetick, tho' I suppose my Father did not know it to be so himself . . . the Tears run down his Face very plentifully' (6). It is hardly possible to suppose that the old man Robinson Crusoe would, except as he has become old, subscribe to the sentiment urged by his father. Nor is it possible to suppose that Defoe himself intends the moral of the book to consist in such elderly simplifications. Instead, and on the contrary, the narrative strategy throws into relief the conflict between civilized and primitive (or 'natural') values that constitutes a theme of the book.

For *Robinson Crusoe* is a perhaps deceptive mixture of narrative and reflection, deceptive in that the two modes are so closely intermixed, the one qualifying the other, and both to be judged as emanating from the pen of an old man whose actions enjoy the support of Daniel Defoe but whose rationalizations of those actions do not always earn his approval. Crusoe's account of his decision not to return to York from London after his harrowing first adventures at sea is representative; he speaks of 'that evil Influence which carryed me first away from my Father's House, that hurried me into the wild and indigested Notion of raising my fortune: and that imprest those Conceits so forcibly upon me as to make me deaf to all good Advice, and to the entreaties and even Command of my Father' (16): these are to be understood as the pieties of an ageing man, whereas his taking ship for Africa is an action to be applauded, assuredly not least because it is a rebellious action.

Later, during the first year of his habitation of the island, the feverish Crusoe has a terrifying dream in which the vengeful

Almighty descends in flames from heaven and says: ' *"Seeing all these Things have not brought thee to Repentance, now thou shalt die:"* At which Words I thought he lifted up the Spear that was in his Hand, to kill me' (87). But everything in the novel serves to justify Crusoe's rebellion from the good instruction of his father. The novel serves as an invitation to define oneself anew, to establish oneself in a context where self-dependence is the hallmark of heroism. In this sense Crusoe's regret expressed here for the lack of what he calls divine knowledge, that is knowledge of God, only underscores the price, or the cost, of heroism. (Compare the other prophetic dream, a dream that comes true [198–99]).

Another capital point should be noticed about the structure of *Robinson Crusoe*. Besides the narrative in retrospect there is also the short-lived Journal, which covers some of the same ground already in the narrative itself. A plausible explanation for the inclusion of the Journal passages is that they are there to make the narrative appear more immediate than it would otherwise be; but the actual impression, I think, is just the opposite. The Journal is exemplary of the dangers of recording with insufficient reflection, objectivity, and detachment the events of daily life. And even the Journal is retrospective: Crusoe does not begin keeping it till he has built himself a table and chair: not until November of 1659 does he turn back to September 30, the day he was shipwrecked. In fact on adjacent pages Crusoe gives two versions of that fateful day (69 and 70). The final Journal version, heavily infused with retrospective didacticism, is clearly the more artful, the more blatantly so as it is the third version of this day to which the reader has been treated; the first and most poignant being that which occurs twenty-four pages earlier (46). Surely the effect of the device of the Journal demonstrates, among other things, the control of the narrator over his materials. By the way, it is indicatively symbolic that Crusoe's ink supply fails him after little more than a year on the island; the true primitive is liberated from dependence on this mode of communication. 'While my Ink lasted,' Crusoe says, 'I kept things very exact, but after that was gone I could not, for I could not make Ink by any Means that I could devise' (65). But, while it does last, the Journal contains retrospects within retrospects, being interlarded with parentheses; and it soon trails off into the generalized narrative that is the typical mode of presentation in this novel.

The hero of this extraordinary epic of the middle class is himself anything but ordinary. He is not even characteristic of the hero of the novel as it developed in the eighteenth century. Usually such a hero begins in conflict with his society, and the narrative that ensues serves to demonstrate the reversal of the course of his rebellion. The eighteenth-century hero ends by becoming thoroughly integrated; he ends by learning prudence, as does Tom Jones, or that self-love and social are the same; success is the outcome of the acquiescence by self-love in the social imperative. Robinson Crusoe is set apart, and that is the point; the very title page tells us that he is 'all *alone* in an *un-inhabited* Island . . . Having been cast on Shore by Shipwreck, wherein all the Men perished but *himself.*' The pleonasm is worthy of a modern politician. And while it may be pointed out (as does Angus Ross in the introduction to the Penguin edition) that Crusoe builds 'a physical and moral replica of the world he had left behind him' [7]), and that he returns to that civilization at last – perfectly reconciled, as he insists, to its norms, even to the extent of preaching them at the reader; despite these accommodations, Crusoe remains an eccentric, an outsider. When he first runs away to sea he discovers his essential loneliness; in the terrifying storm off Yarmouth roads, he 'fell down in a Swoon. As this was a time when every Body had his own Life to think of, no Body minded me, or what was become of me' (12). The focus on the isolated self becomes the point of the novel, especially and most particularly on the island, for there the world Crusoe builds up is of his own making, of his own limits; it is a society without inhabitants, a kingdom without subjects, a state without threatened boundaries. Or so Crusoe thinks for a decade and a half. In this connection it is useful to remember Lemuel Gulliver, whose adventures were being written almost contemporaneously with those of Crusoe; Gulliver's travels take him to one society after another, to that of huge creatures, tiny creatures, odd utopian experimentalists, even rational horses; and in these several societies he encounters a bewildering mixture of what he has left behind in European civilization and what is original and new – and better, or worse. Gulliver's preference at the end of his travels for the company of horses comically underscores the naiveté of a hero whose belief in the capacity for reasonableness is shared by Swift, but whose naiveté is not. Unlike *Robinson Crusoe, Gulliver's Travels* is a profoundly *social* tract.

In more than one way Crusoe is a man without a country. He spends the greater part of his life, and spends it by design, far from his native ground, where anyway he can claim to be but half

English, his father being 'a Foreigner of *Bremen*', and he himself the bearer of an anglicized German surname. Robinson Crusoe is no doubt a deliberately universalized name. His Christian name is associatively yoked with that of Robin the ordinary serving-man (Robin being the name used in Defoe's day for an hostler or other such servant whose name one did not know, and the anglicization, as the hero tells us, of Kreutznaer (4), suggests the pilgrim in him; he bears the sign of the cross in his very name.

Even in society, in Brazil on his plantation, he is an isolate: 'I had no body to converse with but now and then . . . [a] Neighbour; no Work to be done but by the Labour of my Hands; and I used to say I liv'd just like a man cast away upon some desolate Island, that has nobody there but himself' (35). For he chooses to be by himself, even parting willingly with his servant Xury without a pang of regret. Here is the centre of attraction of Crusoe as hero. He dares to be alone, rejoices in his solitude, shuns the company of others. In this way the novel *Robinson Crusoe* nourishes our longings to separate ourselves from all human ties. It caters to our secret antipathy to our fellow creatures, our romantic attachment to alienation, our submerged misanthropy. Was anything more satisfyingly itemized than Crusoe's realization that all his ship-mates have perished, leaving him in possession of his island – 'not one Soul sav'd but my self; for, as for them, I never saw them afterwards, or any Sign of them, except three of their Hats, one Cap, and two Shoes that were not Fellows' (46). And despite occasional expressions of regret for the course his life has taken, Crusoe nearly always succeeds in vanquishing his social longings, for his is a saga of self-dependence, and he recognizes it as such. Shortly after the fourth anniversary of his landing on the island he reflects: 'I look'd now upon the World as a Thing remote, which I had nothing to do with, no Expectation from, and indeed no Desires about' (128). His life, he later says, is 'better than sociable' (135). So thoroughly does he accustom himself to being alone that the celebrated shock of 'the Print of a Man's naked Foot on the Shore' (153) stems from the threat that it offers to the complete and satisfying life that Crusoe has made for himself. Later, it is true, the picture alters somewhat; the shipwreck that takes place near his island fills him with 'a desire after the society of my fellow creatures', but twenty-four years have passed since Crusoe has been cast ashore, and he has learned to live alone. On this point I disagree with Maximillian Novak; Crusoe, he says, 'survives his solitude, but he is always afraid, always cautious. Defoe recognized the benefits of the state of nature, but he believed that the freedom and purity of Crusoe's island were minor advantages compared to the comfort and security of civilization' (Novak 1963, 22). The evidence, which assuredly can be taken in more than one way, appears to me to favour the heroism of solitude; Crusoe requires the manageable dimensions of a small island. Great Britain is manifestly too large for him; and he needs loneliness. On the overland return from Lisbon to England, Crusoe experiences the terror of a crossing of the Pyrenees, and there is a justification for it in that he and his party encounter wolves, a bear, and killing snow (292). I think it is right to say that the Pyrenees episode is particularly horrifying to Crusoe because he is no longer isolated, no longer protected by the boundaries of an island; he is in a world without limits and in an environment he cannot control.

Likewise the ending of the novel is no ending; it is a conclusion in which nothing is concluded, for all the world in this respect like the picaresque tale, in which more of the same is promised beyond the end of the last page. There is no tidiness of marriage and living happily ever after; indeed, convention is turned on its head by the introduction and then dismissal of that honourable formula, which I want to turn to shortly.

The ultimate test of Crusoe's preference for isolatedness must be made by considering his regard for the other persons in his life. For one thing, the other characters in the book are nearly all nameless, even Crusoe's own brothers and his own wife and children. His parents are named only in so far as they give their names to Robinson Crusoe. Crusoe has a friend who arranges the first voyage that he undertakes, but this friend is never named. Nor is the captain who befriends him on the first voyage to African waters. Nor that captain's widow, who looks after his money for many years. While certain characters, especially unimportant characters, do bear surnames or first names (but almost never both), the usual designation is 'one of my companions' or 'the master of a ship' and the like. Friday is so called because Crusoe encounters him on that day of the week. Nor are any of the characters, except Crusoe himself, particularized – even Friday, whose comic patois is a mere cartoon of primitivism. I agree with James Sutherland that 'Friday is not much more to Crusoe than a higher sort of dog' (xiii).

And Crusoe cheerfully – or at least unregretfully – parts with all who are near and evidently dear to him. He sells Xury for sixty pieces of eight, he sends Friday back to the mainland, his own wife and children are summarily dismissed as follows: 'I marry'd, and that not either to my Disadvantage or Dissatisfaction, and had three Children, two Sons and one Daughter: But my Wife dying, and my Nephew coming Home with good Success from a Voyage to *Spain*, my inclination to go Abroad, and his Importunity, prevailed and engag'd me to go in his Ship, as a private Trader to the *East Indies'* (305). Indeed his regard for human life other than his own is such that he proposes shooting two of the mutineers who have landed on his island – whereas the captain of the ship on which the mutiny has taken place resists such a brutal solution, though he has been taken prisoner and ill-treated by these men (256); and there is nothing to choose between Crusoe's regard for Xury and that for Friday.

Robinson Crusoe is a sublunary epic of disobedience, the consequences of which are comic rather than tragic, a Paradise Found of the middle class. It is a domestic saga of foreign adventure, in which the more it changes the more it becomes the same thing; Crusoe's island is a little England, a kingdom even so called, over which Crusoe avowedly reigns. It is complete with castle, cave, and grot – though for a long time without subjects, except goats and a parrot. The narrative is organized around its hero's disobedience, a fortunate fall indeed. To Kreutznaer senior the fatherhood of the family is not symbolic of the fatherhood of God, nor is it to his son Robinson. Therefore I should want to argue that the religious musings in the novel are wholly exterior to the force that moves the hero. Despite what some readers have urged, Robinson Crusoe's mode of existence, for all the apparatus of Puritanism and for all the old-man's pieties that interlard the narrative, is unconvincing as a religious tract. Ian Watt is no doubt right as well as charitable when he says that Crusoe's 'spiritual intentions were probably quite sincere, but they have the weakness of all "Sunday religion" and manifest themselves in somewhat unconvincing periodic tributes to the transcendent at times when a respite from real action and practical intellectual effort is allowed or enforced' (81).

Toward Crusoe as *homo economicus,* which is the observation of Karl Marx and the argument of Ian Watt, I am much more sympathetic than I am to the view that he is a man whose experiences constitute a saga whose end is divine revelation. As Watt argues, 'Crusoe's "original sin" is really the dynamic tendency of capitalism itself, whose aim is never merely to maintain the *status quo*, but to transform it incessantly. Leaving home, improving the lot one was born to, is a vital feature in the individualist pattern of life' (67–68). Yet Crusoe is never driven by economic necessity. His father is well enough off to be retired as a merchant and altogether willing to help him get started in business. So the reader is told at the beginning of the book. But Crusoe has 'a wild and indigested Notion of raising my Fortune' (16). He wants to succeed on his own. Nor does it go unnoticed that when he goes off to Africa at this point he does not ship as a sailor but as a passenger; he can afford to do so. As a speculator he thrives from the beginning. His four years in Brazil are highly remunerative and he could remain there for a lifetime – but from there he goes off to Africa to make another fortune in the slave trade. He is, if you like, a hero of capitalist enterprise with the restraints removed. He is liberated from economic struggle in part by his own effort, in part by luck. Improvidence is his watchword; he has no need for financial security, and he does not want such security. He wants the world on his own terms, and he gets his wish. At one moment of delectable self-satisfaction – it is not the only one – he says of his perfect self-sufficiency on his island: 'I was remov'd from all the Wickedness of the World here. I had neither *the Lust of the Flesh, the Lust of the Eye, or the Pride of Life.* I had nothing to covet; for I had all that I was now capable of enjoying; I was Lord of the whole Mannor; or if I pleas'd I might call my self King or Emperor over the whole Country which I had Possession of. There were no Rivals; I had no Competitor, none to dispute Sovereignty or Command with me' (128). This is at the end of the fourth year – and he has two more decades of isolated bliss to enjoy before having to face up to human relationships again. When he does have to do so, his 'subjects,' as he calls them, are his creatures completely. 'I was absolute Lord and Lawgiver', (241) he says of Friday and Friday's father, and the Spaniard rescued from those who were about to cook and eat him. To be sure, at the end of the novel, Crusoe returns to England, though not for long – he is soon off again. In a way *The Farther Adventures of Robinson Crusoe* and the *Serious Reflections* serve to confirm the importance of the heroism of megalomania, the former at no point capturing the excitement of the original, the latter as an all but unreadable series of banal reflections. Crusoe's very success justifies both his first disobedience and his recklessly rugged individualism.

Robinson Crusoe succeeds where everyone else must fail; by sheer force of will and animal spirits and ingenuity he creates a whole world, all alone. He is the only free man, and he gives all his readers a glimpse of what it would be like to be really free, if dreams could come true, if the ego (or rather the id) were all. *Robinson Crusoe* lays bare one of the most elemental and savage facts of all, that of egocentric impulse against the apparatus of society, and in society's despite. Novak says, rightly: 'For all the time spent discussing the realism of *Robinson Crusoe*, we would miss everything if we did not feel the force behind the hero's daydreams' (Novak 1983, 46).

There is something defiantly, though no doubt unconsciously, atavistic about Robinson Crusoe. He evades classification as gingerly as though he were attempting to avoid being caught; he tries to escape from the civilizations, man-made and self-made, that would contain him; he runs from them, and with equally glorious incaution, from himself. The ultimate regression is death, and Robinson Crusoe's journey surely points to that destination. This saga of do-it-yourselfishness concludes, however, on a cheerful and forward-looking note; in fantasy, death has no more than a temporary sting, and the dreamer awakens with a future still to be enjoyed.

So *Robinson Crusoe* does not really end, it trails off, rather rosily; and here it differs from the picaresque tale. Lazarillo de Tormes's discovery of the perdurability of hunger is the reverse of rosy; the tentativeness of all the young man's arrangements is a matter for defiance, even for confidence, based on his past successes, such as they have been; but Robinson Crusoe is *rich*, as well as assured, though restless. Certainly he has not arrived at any point of finality, either in his own mind or in the mind of his creator. And to meditate on what is now rather fashionably called the closure of *Robinson Crusoe* is to see that it occupies a position somewhere between that of the picaresque tale and the well-made plot of which *Tom Jones* is the example of examples. Fredric Jameson has said: 'Our satisfaction with the completeness of plot is . . . a kind of satisfaction with society as well, which has through the very possibility of such an ordering of events revealed itself to be a coherent totality, and one with which for the moment, the individual unit, the individual human life itself, is not in contradiction' (12). Accordingly, it is possible to see in the plotting of *Robinson Crusoe* the sense of what may be called dissatisfied hope – but hope indeed – which is the hallmark of the second decade of the eighteenth century in England, and indeed the hallmark of Defoe himself.

If we learn to behave as Robinson Crusoe says he learned to behave, all will be well for us. If we are young we will return to our fathers, and content ourselves with the middle state. If we are older, and have been guilty like Robinson of rebelling against paternal authority, we can at least do what Robinson does or said he did on his island – we can reflect on the consequences of our disobedience, and by way of that more or less traumatic series of reflections, repent, and be led to confess our sin of disobedience, and put ourselves in the hands of a merciful God. Such is the narrative's indulgence in plain hope, but few of this novel's readers will be satisfied to stop there; and I do not think that great subtlety is required to observe that there is a contrapuntal theme as well; all readers of this novel must feel the covert sense in which the narrative is to be taken, countering the pieties of the overt theme, insisting on the absolute centrality of self-love, at the willing expense of all other creatures, human and otherwise. In this sense, as I am by no means the first to claim (Richetti and Alkon likewise find this dimension in the book), *Robinson Crusoe* goes beyond the ideological to the mythical, the potency of which puts Defoe in the company of Shakespeare and Cervantes; and if he was never again to achieve so much, his masterpiece remains to console its readers for their self-absorption, and rebuke them for their incapacity to love themselves nonetheless.

II *THE MOSQUITO COAST:* ISOLATION AS MADNESS

The Mosquito Coast is a version of *Robinson Crusoe* written in the twilight of the American Dream, a defiant and fiercely sympathetic look at the shape of American culture as the twentieth century draws to a close. There is no sanction of the free-enterprising and regardless selfishness of that dream, but there is substantiation of the dream's generosity, resourcefulness, and courage, which in Allie Fox, the father of the narrator, has gone disastrously, crazily wrong. If it is really true, as he says, that 'No one loves this country more than I do. . . . And that's why I'm going. Because I can't bear to watch' (67), he must in this respect be sharply differentiated from

Robinson Crusoe, who has no patriotic feelings, except those of mere sentimentality. Charlie Fox, the narrator of *The Mosquito Coast*, is a thirteen-year-old boy – or rather, the narration begins when he is thirteen; for, like *Robinson Crusoe*, *The Mosquito Coast* is a retrospective account, and it could not have been written unless Charlie had learned and survived the bitter lessons of the defeat and death of his father in Honduras, liberating Charlie and the other members of his family so that they can return to America and take up the threads, slender though they are, of a civilization which is interdependent rather than self-dependent.

Paul Theroux sorts out this myth as an insider; and, beside his hero, Robinson Crusoe looks crudely naive, though only at first glance. The fact is that Crusoe is no more naive than Allie; Allie is so in the way provided and permitted by the highly-developed technological society that he tries to flee from, unsuccessfully in the event; whereas Crusoe has a more accurate sense of how to make life work in accordance with the bourgeois practices that he takes along with him to the island.

At the beginning of *Robinson Crusoe* the young hero has been urged by his father to accept the middle state into which he has been born, and to choose a life of commerce that will be safe and productive and therefore proper as well as profitable. But Robinson, though he declares many years later that he regrets not having listened to his father, is driven by the spirit of adventure and of independence, to take ship and go wandering. By contrast, Charlie Fox, the son of his father, is utterly dominated by Allie Fox, frightened of him, dependent on him, unable to contemplate any alternative to doing exactly what his father asks him to do, and promptly.

Indeed it is one of the strengths of *The Mosquito Coast* that Allie Fox is seen through the eyes of Charlie; the reader sees more and better than Charlie sees, through Allie Fox to the crazed autodidact, the obsessed megalomaniac, that he really is; and because Charlie does not see all these things, the reader sees Charlie the better, understands his opacities, his immaturity – and looks to him for what happens in the novel. From one viewpoint *The Mosquito Coast* is Allie Fox's story; but it is even more centrally the story of Charlie Fox and the modification of his vision of life. And when at the end of the novel he and his family return to the civilization that Allie Fox has rejected, the last word is understood to be not disillusionment but hope.

The existence of such alternatives helps to place *The Mosquito Coast* historically: they do not exist in *Robinson Crusoe*, a Renaissance work if there ever was one, in which the world lies open to conquest, in which mastery is possible, and defeat, though not unthinkable, is too distant to be much of a threat. More narrowly, *The Mosquito Coast* can be seen as a commentary on the 1960s in America, with its ideological collisions, exacerbated by the Vietnam war, leading to a fundamentalist primitivism that is harrowingly depicted in the novel.

Another way of placing the novel historically is to look at its other literary forebears, the most obvious and prominent of which are *Huckleberry Finn* and *Heart of Darkness*, though *The Swiss Family Robinson* should also be looked at briefly, because it too finds a place in *The Mosquito Coast*.

The Mosquito Coast reeks of *Huckleberry Finn*, at first because of the nearness in age and naiveté of the narrators; both works are about the ending of innocence, and the acquisition of such knowledge of the world as will make the world livable after all. But Huck is supposed to be illiterate, and there is a sense in which the narrative itself of *Huckleberry Finn* is presented as moment-to-moment; it hardly looks backward. Charlie Fox is a literate youth, and he is firmly in possession of a retrospect that is unmistakably a retrospect. He knows before the beginning of the story he tells all the truth about his father, and he shapes the narrative so that the revelation will come to the reader as it came to him; or, more exactly, he tells the story in such a way as to show that the revelation came to him as the confirmation of certain suspicions or doubts that he has had all along. But the operation of dramatic irony, the superior knowledge that the readers of his tale have over Charlie Fox as observed within the narrative, enforce the acquisition of knowledge at a faster rate than Charlie's rate. There are hints and more than hints from the beginning that Charlie's father is not the infallible creature that he is assumed to be by Charlie. In addition, it is instructive to look at the spiritual distance between *Huckleberry Finn* and *The Mosquito Coast*; Twain's world appears, innocently from its author's viewpoint, to offer happiness as an ideal in a world that still provides stability against which to pit rectitude and freedom. By contrast, Theroux's dedication of *The Mosquito Coast* to 'Charlie Fox' – in quotation marks – requires that the not-very-covert allusion to the Vietnam War summon up dark recollections about the recent American past.

Yet another book behind *The Mosquito Coast* is *Heart of Darkness* (Theroux himself has written a *Heart of Darkness* novel, *Jungle Lovers*, but I do not want to consider it here; good though it is, it has not the stature of *The Mosquito Coast*). Conrad's masterpiece comes to the mind of the reader of Theroux's novel because of the resemblance between Allie and Kurtz; both megalomaniacs, both intensely self-absorbed even to the commission of murder in the effort to bend the world to their wills. But it is a measure of the gap between Conrad and Theroux, as well as a measure of the eight decades that separate their two books, that Kurtz in his mad way seeks to bring civilization to the interior of Africa, among the savages whom he comes increasingly to resemble. Moreover Allie Fox, though he has a mesmerizing voice and manner as well, seeks the opposite of Kurtz; he seeks a primitive state stripped of civilization, while at the same time he is dependent on and indeed wedded to that civilization. Nor does Allie, even at the desperate end of his adventure, seek to cross any lines in an effort to associate himself with the primitive rhythms and primitive knowledge of those who dwell in central Honduras. Allie Fox hates K-Marts and Holiday Inns and hamburgers; but he loves to smoke cigars and tinker with an Evinrude outboard motor and build a giant refrigerator in the jungle. Compelled by his own inventiveness because (as he sardonically puts it) he thinks of it as an antidote to the botched job left undone by God, he is as much a prisoner of the civilization that he flees as are the people he flees from – more so than some, more than his own children, who are able to make at Jeronimo a natural oasis that is not within the imaginative grasp of their father. And they save him, though only temporarily, at the crisis, for no-one can ultimately save him from himself.

When Allie is about to buy the village of Jeronimo in Honduras he says, 'We're not the Swiss Family Robinson' (109). By this he means that he and his family are not afloat on a journey around the world, rather mindlessly tossed from one coast to another, but rather that they have chosen to settle in a particular place, selected for its richness of possibility. Also, the Fox family is not weighed down or inspired by the faith that marks every step of the journey taken by the Robinsons. The Swiss Family Robinson is a collection of pious Crusoes; Allie Fox is defiantly impious: he not only fails to trust the Lord, he scorns those who do. On the more than merely tramplike freighter that takes them from Baltimore to La Ceiba, the difficulties that the ship encounters in the tropical storm, the listing and the yawing that the Captain seems unable to put right himself, these difficulties are dealt with by Allie Fox, who with his tool kit goes below and in a few hours makes the necessary adjustments. It is a matter of engineering rather than faith, though the terrible missionary family aboard the ship – they are the Spellgoods – try to pray themselves out of the danger. Allie Fox's triumph is a victory in God's despite, of defiant lucidity over miasmic petition. The fact that Allie can out-quote the Reverend Mr Spellgood even in biblical matters only adds to the sense of triumph.

It is surely no accident that the North American setting of *The Mosquito Coast* is the state of the union that contains Thoreau's pond, and that Allie Fox, who comes from Maine, is a quintessential Yankee. Recognising Allie at once as the somewhat outsize version of what are supposed to be the best Yankee traits, outsize to the point of caricature, we are nonetheless drawn to him because of the wonderful clarity with which he sees the dilapidation of what is good in the American Dream, the erosion of self-reliance, the disappearance of whatever was made by hand and made with pride, the depersonalization not only of New England but of the USA altogether. That New England itself has been invaded by flimsy plastic sleeping bags imported from Taiwan; that migrant workers must be brought from Central America, indeed from the very Honduras into which Allie wishes to take his family in order to turn his back on the ruins of a civilization that is nostalgically evoked; that the schools should serve up pap in the way of courses in Communication consisting of sessions in front of a television set; that Harvard College – Harvard! – should turn out physical and intellectual weaklings: all these deepen the sense of estrangement that Allie knows, and the readers of the book are obviously intended to feel a sympathetic sense of estrangement themselves.

The Fox family mother almost never contests her husband's orders; she contents herself to remain in ignorance of what he intends doing; she does not reprove him; she teaches her children without preaching to them; she understands much more of nature than does Allie; she can name the trees, and see the landscape, and show her children how to look. Charlie, the elder of the sons is more aware of the shape of reality than his younger brother Jerry. At the same time he is the more his father's prisoner than is Jerry. Charlie tries to believe that his father is never wrong, however much suffering may be inflicted on the son by the father. Even in the teeth of evidence that he would prefer not to evaluate, he wills omniscience in his father, and there is a strong Oedipal motif in *The Mosquito Coast*. Jerry, however, is not so illusioned, and so he manages to make remarks of acidulous frankness; he hates his father, and knows he hates him. The twin daughters, Clover and April – aged five – know more than they should for their age, and are exhibited by their father as the triumph of keeping children out of school, for in Allie Fox's opinion, schools are less than useless; they are positively baneful.

In Massachusetts, the Foxes have been dependent on a man who is a somewhat grotesque fulfilment of the Horatio Alger story – an immigrant called Polski, who has made enough of a success as a farmer to be able to hire the Hondurans who live on his farm; successful enough also to be able to buy his wife a mink coat that he keeps in the cooling room in which cut asparagus is stored. By the standards of Allie Fox, Polski is a successful entrepreneur. But compared to Allie, Polski is a pale version of a familiar picture; for even as an anti-dreamer Allie is an extreme case. He looks back to a time, about a century ago, before America became 'a dope-taking, door-locking, ulcerated danger zone of rabid scavengers and criminal millionaires and moral sneaks' (3). The hyperbole commands not only attention but also respect. And coupled to the case against America is the strongly apocalyptic note struck by Allie as his *leitmotiv*: 'I'm the last man' (6). One of the elements in the vision of Allie is his sense of post-apocalyptic thinking. He dreams of his new-made civilization at Jeronimo because he has already become convinced that the United States and indeed the whole of the civilized world is doomed. To make something out of the wreckage is the true and greatest challenge. That Jeronimo had been a settlement and had been abandoned by the man who sold it to him *satisfies* Allie as nothing else could do. Education, he says, should be 'not writing poetry, or fingerpainting, or what's the capital of Texas – but survival, rebuilding a civilization from the smoking ruins' (148–49).

Allie is a curious but by no means unique kind of American intellectual. He dropped out of Harvard though he had gone there on a scholarship from the Maine fishing village in which he had grown up, disillusioned prematurely by the restrictive boundaries of the academy – as were Thoreau and likewise Henry James. And Allie took the primitivistic direction of Thoreau; *The Mosquito Coast* is a critique of primitivism in that the author chooses to present

Allie in the role of an inventor who thinks himself to be a kind of god – who, ironically, introduces into the ecosystem (a word that Allie himself uses) an alien element, ignoring the rhythm of the universe. For, prescient of the disastrous ice house in Honduras, the prototype of the catastrophic giant refrigerator, is the kerosene-fuelled machine that Allie constructs for the migrant workers on Polski's farm. Moreover, the irony is not lost even on Allie that the Honduran migrants and he are changing places. Miserably paid though they are on Polski's farm, miserably housed as well, they do not want to return to their native land. It is an irony also that though they are ignorant, even illiterate, they know better than Allie the difficulties of Honduran life.

Obviously he has become more and more obsessed, more and more megalomaniacal, more and more sure that he is the last man because the world is coming to an end, and that he will be among the first to die because 'they always kill the smart ones first – the ones they're afraid will outwit them' (16–17). So the making of the Worm Tub even before the Fox family leaves New England pre-figures the monstrous Fat Boy of the Honduran wilderness. 'Ice,' Allie says, 'is civilization' (32). Why does he think so? He thinks so because he is a prisoner of his own inventiveness; he imagines that engineering skill, that mechanism, that technical adeptness, is a more fully encompassing force for good than it is; in this respect Allie is a prisoner of the twentieth-century dream which is by no means exclusively American – nor (if one dare say it) by no means exclusively bad. Nonetheless, it must not be forgotten that the name given to the bomb dropped on Nagasaki on 9 August 1945 was called 'Fat Boy'.[4]

When Allie says that ice is civilization he is thinking of the term in what for him is its ameliorative sense. Later, in Honduras, he explains what ice can do. Ice can freeze fish, it can act as an anaesthetic, and so forth. But these are not 'natural' triumphs, they are technological applications. Such is the confusion that afflicts his mind: he cannot steer his way between the shoals – K-Marts and

---

[4] 'At 8.15 A. M., August 6, [Colonel Paul W.] Tibbets released over Hiroshima a uranium bomb of the type called "Little Boy". He reported later: "As far as I was concerned it was a perfect operation". On August 9, a plutonium bomb known as "Fat Boy" was dropped on Nagasaki. The destruction in each case exceeded the most careful extrapolations of scientists, and it was hours before the mushroom clouds, smoke, and flames had sufficiently blown away to permit adequate photo-reconnaisance.' (Sulzberger 590).

Holiday Inns and hamburgers are civilization in its pejorative sense; the ice-making mechanism, however, is good. Not until after he has incinerated the three white invaders of Jeronimo in Fat Boy does he correctly assess his failure to discriminate. When he acknowledges that he has done wrong to use poisons and explosives to cause his ice house to function, he resolves, as he says, to confine himself in future to physics rather than chemistry. But even at this point he remains a tinkerer, a god who will remake the world.

Obviously enough, Allie is longing for a past that never existed and that therefore never can be recaptured. What Allie looks back to is a humanity that is uncontaminated, and that is amenable to technological development in such a way as never to corrupt those whom it benefits. Allie does not see two things: neither the double-edged advantages of technological advancement nor the face of nature herself. The failure is clearly depicted in the rescue that Charlie performs on the night in Jeronimo when Fat Boy erupts, broken apart by the trapped interlopers, who manage to bring destruction on the whole of Jeronimo as they try to fight their way out of the trap of Fat Boy itself, in which they have been barricaded by Allie; he has caused them to die because with their weapons they threaten the stability of Jeronimo. Allie destroys it, building by building, in order to save it; *The Mosquito Coast* was written after Vietnam. But Charlie leads his family, including Allie himself, to the Acre for shelter and rest and protection.

There is much omitted, too much, in Allie's primitivism – it is a shorn primitivism, a narrowly egomaniacal view. Thus, in the flush of his early triumph at Jeronimo, before the dream has turned sour, he reflects on the Zambus approvingly: 'They don't paint pictures, they don't weave baskets or carve faces on coconuts or hollow out salad bowls. They don't sing or dance or write poems. They can't draw a straight line. That's why I like them. That's innocence. They're a little touched with religion, but they'll get over that. Mother, there's hope here' (149).

But from the beginning Charlie has the sense of loss that stems from his not being able to associate with others of his own age. Allie does not believe in sending his children to school, and so encounters difficulties with the truant officers, who know perfectly well that the Fox children are being kept away by their father. And when Charlie sees his contemporaries, ordinary children of Hatfield, Massachusetts, returning from school on their bicycles, chattering companionably, and ready to jeer at the likes of the Foxes, he envies them. He is ashamed, as he acknowledges later, of being different from them. He envies his father for being free as he himself cannot be free, and he 'hated [himself] for feeling ashamed' (34). To Allie school means 'sniffing glue in the schoolyard, boasting about their toys, looking at pictures, raising hell. Watching TV – that's all they do in school' (34). Yet Charlie is to be proved right, and his father wrong. That is to say, Charlie's return to North America at the end of the novel after Allie's death is an acknowledgment that Allie's past cannot be recaptured because it was never there – it was always imaginary; *The Mosquito Coast* shows up the Crusoe longings of Allie Fox and turns the reader toward a civilization that is far from ideal, far from satisfactory, but that besides being inescapable is also preferable to the sentimental primitivism that takes the Fox family from New England to Honduras.

So *The Mosquito Coast* insists that its readers understand the larger picture as corrective. In this sense it is politically aware in offering indictment of the superstructure that controls the America of the 1980s. But the political implications of the creation of Allie Fox fail to suggest that you cannot go home again. On the contrary, you can flee neither the masterpieces nor the nightmares; what has been created cannot be undone though perhaps it will be destroyed. For Allie destruction is preferable to trying to accommodate oneself to what mankind has made – but Allie Fox is crazy, and he becomes more so as the novel progresses. *The Mosquito Coast* exhibits the futility of nihilism, the destructiveness of the primitivistic urge if taken too far. The novel offers hope.

On the beach near the ship on which the family is to sail to Honduras, Allie inflicts a test on Charlie that is characteristic. There, in Baltimore, on a strip of sand strewn with broken glass, Charlie must go out in the cold water and perch on a rock until the tide washes over him, and wait until his father calls him in. It is an endurance test, which Charlie must face repeatedly. There is soon to be another one, the climbing of the rigging of the ship, much to the dismay of the captain, who sends a crew member up to rescue the boy. Then there is the most gothic test of all, in which Charlie is made to enter the giant refrigerator's maze of greasy pipes in near darkness. But always he does what his father orders him to do, and almost always without demur.

On the beach in Baltimore, he recognizes, though only for a

moment, the separateness and strangeness of his father. 'He was dark. I did not know him, and he watched me like a stranger, with curiosity rather than affection. And I felt like a stranger to him. We were two people pausing – one on a rock, the other on the sand, child and adult. I did not know him, he did not know me. I had to wait to discover who we were' (66). Here is a fine blending of recollection of what the moment felt like at the time it was experienced, and what in retrospect Charlie feels about that moment as he can perceive its meaning from a distance. Then, a couple of paragraphs later: 'Now I could see Father's face. A wildness passed across it, like a desperate memory, making a mad fix on his jaw.' The boy could see the wildness then, when he was a boy of thirteen; the man who is writing *The Mosquito Coast,* or ostensibly writing it, can now discern something of the meaning of that wildness, and communicate it to the reader with touching precision.

On board the ship to La Ceiba is the missionary family who will play a crucial role in the lives of the Foxes in Honduras. They are the philoprogenitive Reverend Gurney Spellgood and his family of nine. Irresistibly Allie pours scorn on him and his prayers for the righting of the listing ship. But it is an irony that very much later in Honduras it will be their 'civilization' that will help make possible the earthly salvation that the Foxes will so urgently need. And it will be the chinless Spellgood daughter who will give Charlie the beginnings of a sexual awakening.

Allie Fox views the Bible as 'an owner's guide . . . for Western civilization. But it doesn't work. I started wondering. Where's the problem? Is it us or is it the handbook?' (77). This view makes possible the setting up of Allie Fox by himself to be a god that will not fail, the author so to speak of an owner's manual that tells how things should be rightly ordered: Allie's view of the Bible is, in other words, a blueprint for his own self-exaltation. Like William Blake, Allie Fox says, 'Man is God' (87), and he believes the utterance, just as Blake does – but Blake had gone on to say: 'Thy own humanity learn to adore' (*The Everlasting Gospel,* 76). Blake is a natural believer, in at least two senses of the word natural; Allie is by way of being a village atheist, determined to prove the non-existence of God, displacing Him with an arrogance the dangers of which he never fully recognizes, even at the end of his life.

The second section of *The Mosquito Coast* takes the Fox family through the mainly formative experiences of the Honduran settlement, up to and including the explosion and destruction of the ice house, and the ruin that is visited on the settlement at Jeronimo. It begins with the vultures that hang about the harbour of La Ceiba: 'I hate those birds', Allie says (105); they have a strongly symbolic value for him not only because they are beyond the boundary of his possible control, but because he too is a kind of vulture, and he dimly recognizes this fact – for instance when he goes to the dump with Charlie to collect bits and pieces of scrap metal and wheels and wire with which to make his contrivances, the parallel is patent; Allie is a technological vulture who will come to be eaten by his natural counterparts.

From the beginning of the arrival at La Ceiba, Charlie longs for home. The rusty old banana boat on which they have sailed to Central America is also a symbol, for all its dilapidated condition, of what they have had to give up. 'That ship was my hope' (110). Later: 'The disappearance of the white ship left me feeling helpless and half blind, as if a handy thing had been tricked out of my head. It was hope. I had felt safe because the ship had been there – we could go home. Now I felt abandoned' (118). And Jerry, the younger brother, always the more frank, says of La Ceiba, 'It's junk, it stinks, it's crappo. I hate it.'

Since this is Charlie's story, it is well to realize that even at this point the boy is in search of a father – because, as he will discover, Allie Fox is so completely absorbed that his children and eventually even his wife are the instruments of his will; and he punishes them terribly when they dare to question or balk at his authority. Still, Charlie 'believed everything he said' (128) – because the alternative would be despair, and Charlie has to live with hope, though he does not sort out these feelings at the time he is experiencing them.

Allie declares at the beginning that Jeronimo is beautiful because he has a vision of self-sufficiency, not because he can actually see beauty before his eyes. But he has brought the apparatus of civilization with him: tools and blow-torches and pipes and – most important of all – his engineer's adeptness. Already there, and already suggesting to Charlie the resemblances that assuredly do not occur to his father, are the much-reduced Roper family. 'This family too was a father, a mother, and four children. But the smallest child was naked and being carried like a knapsack by one of the girls. They were our reflections – shrunken shadows of us' (139). It may be doubted whether Charlie was as fully conscious then of the parallel as when later he is supposed to be relating the events set forth in *The Mosquito Coast*.

So while Charlie has misgivings, and the reader of his story even deeper doubts, Jeronimo becomes what Allie has envisioned, complete to the last detail. The land is cleared, the dwellings built, the Burpee seeds planted, the great ice house constructed. Surely one of the appeals in the narrative here is to the primitivistic instincts not in Allie Fox but in the reader. Here, accordingly, is a primordial root or knot that binds *Robinson Crusoe* to *The Mosquito Coast*. The success of the appeal lies in the thoroughness with which the transformation is described and detailed. In Defoe's novel it is notably convincing: likewise in Theroux's. Theroux has learned what it is like to make a life in the jungle; he is convincingly particular in his description of the successful effort by Allie to make such a civilization, including a knowledge of the mechanism of the ice house, the engineering involved, as well as the chemistry of refrigeration. Significantly, Allie cannot make his ice house operate until he has brought, with great effort, ammonia and hydrogen, which he has had to buy with money, from a supplier in Trujillo.

Only halfway through *The Mosquito Coast* the state of perfection has been reached, and there are few portents that disturb the vision of Allie. An intruder, a religious intruder to boot, one Mr Struss, is driven away by Allie. He will return later, and cause more than trouble. For Allie has the proudly self-assertive arrogance to believe that he can be a successful Frankenstein. There is a plausibility, an all-American plausibility, in Allie's declamations in this period. 'Father went on to say that savagery was seeing and not believing you could do it yourself, and that that was a fearful condition. The man who saw a bird and made it into a god, because he could not imagine flying himself, was a savage of the most basic kind' (165–66). As if to confirm Allie's judgement, the interior of the ice house does resemble a human being, so much so that when Charlie has to ascend its innards, among all the pipes that his father has so ingeniously put together, he thinks he has a vision of the inside of his father's mind: 'Father's head, the mechanical part of his brain and the complications of his mind . . . strong and huge and mysterious. It was all revealed to me, but there was too much of it, like a book page full of secrets, printed too small' (168).

In contrast to Allie is Charlie's mother, who learns from the Indians how to skin animals and dry fish and smoke meat. In this respect Charlie and his brother and the Maywit-Ropers are much closer to her than they are to Allie, for on the Acre, so called, they make a refuge that is entirely based on the knowledge acquired from example and also from observation and experiment. But they co-operate with the environment, while Allie takes it to pieces, or tries to, in order to reshape it to his will. It is Charlie himself who is the inspiration for and the leader of the Acre (178), and there the children invent or re-invent all the things which Allie has left behind. They have money, made of stones and pebbles; they have a school and even a church; they make a telephone out of halves of a coconut. They have secrets, and the Acre itself is a secret from Allie. They dig man traps. 'We had not brought a boatload of tools and seeds, and we had not invented anything. We just lived like monkeys' (178). The Acre is a reaction to the vision of Allie's mind that Charlie had within the giant refrigerator. 'In Fat Boy I had seen Father's mind – a version of it – its riddle and slant and its hugeness – and it had scared me' (179–80).

As soon as Fat Boy begins to produce ice, Allie becomes a missionary himself; he declares that he wants to take ice to 'the hottest, darkest, nastiest corner of Honduras, where they pray for water and never see ice, and have never heard of cans, much less aerosol cans' (179). For in his search for a society that has been uncontaminated by civilization, Allie proposes to go to the interior village settlement of Seville, which he believes to be just what he is seeking – rather like the ultimate primitivistic locus of Alejo Carpentier's *Los Pasos perdidos,* except that the hero of that extraordinary novel does actually find such a cradle of civilization. He learns from it. He learns that, having become civilized himself, he cannot live away from what civilization has to offer, namely urbanity and libraries and concerts and picture-galleries and intellectual exchange. Allie wants to take ice to Seville, and he does so, but finds the experience disillusioning in that there are to be found in the place the remains of a flashlight battery, and dwellers who speak a mixture of Spanish and English and Creole – even that the head man wears a bicycle clip on each wrist. Worse: this man provides a version of the Lord's Prayer – 'Ah, Fadder wart neven hello bead name. . . .' (197). These villagers have been visited by missionaries; in his view the quest is accordingly a failure.

The next effort in this direction is much farther away, across the mountains to what Allie hopes will really be an ur-civilization. The account of this trek is one of the finest in *The Mosquito Coast;* and its consequences spell doom to Allie's aspirations, though of course he does not know it at the time. Allie was successful in taking ice to Seville; but when he goes on the second journey, the ice melts, and the last sliver turns to water before it can be shown to the inhabitants of this distant settlement, where there are three white men who appear to be slaves of the fierce and unfriendly Indians who dwell there. What Allie does not realize, because the three white men utterly deceive him, is that they are the true masters, that they have enslaved the Indians, and that they will make their way to Jeronimo, where they will insist on remaining. Later, it is these three, with their guns, whom Allie will imprison in Fat Boy, and who bring about its destruction as well as their own. Allie is their murderer.

At the peak of his pride in his accomplishment, when Fat Boy is working and Jeronimo is tamed, Allie identifies himself directly with the Creator: 'You feel a little like God', he whispered, looking around. . . . 'God had fun making things like icebergs and volcanos. Too bad he didn't finish the job. Ha!' (211). Thus he speaks on the eve of his crossing the mountains; but his days of so speaking are limited.

In the remote Heart of Darkness, the Indians live in misery and degradation, in ruined dwellings with starved dogs, obviously racked by disease and rendered all but helpless by hunger. The place is called Olancho (there is an Olanchito in Honduras). The head Indian says, 'Go away' – and in Spanish! (229). So Allie has not found the cradle of civilization after all, and when the three white men also urge them to clear out, he and his party realize that there is no alternative. But – and it is an unintentionally fatal slip – when Allie and his party leave, Allie tells the white men where Jeronimo is and how to get there.

At this point Charlie's disillusionment about his father comes sharply into focus when Allie lies. There had been no ice when Allie arrived at the Indian settlement, yet Allie pretends on the return journey that there had been, and that the Indians had been flabbergasted. This is a necessary step in the maturation of Charlie Fox; always afterward he is much more wary of accepting and trusting and believing his father, even though Allie does not maintain the lie on his return to Jeronimo; indeed he admits to his wife that the ice has melted.

But there is trouble. The Maywits are gone, carried off by the missionary Mr Struss, whom Allie had sent packing earlier. Mr Struss had called Allie a communist. As usual Allie pretends not to be surprised.

'None of this is news to me,' he said. 'But I'll tell you something you don't know. They'll be back, as sure as anything. Because this is a happy place, and the world isn't. The world is plain rotten. People are mean, they're cruel, they're fake, they always pretend to be something they're not. They're weak. They take advantage. A cruddy, cruddy little man who sees God in a snake, or the devil in thunder, will take you prisoner if he gets the drop on you. Give anyone half a chance and he'll make you a slave: he'll tell you the most awful lies. I've seen them, running around bollocky, playing God. And our friends, the Maywits . . . they'll be lonely out there. They'll be scared, because the world stinks.' (242)

So Allie does not believe in the nobility of civilized persons, but he can hardly be said to believe in the nobility of savages either. By comparison, the world of *Robinson Crusoe* is if not more benign at least more neutral, more amenable, more yielding; Crusoe is able to exploit it because it is exploitable.

After the débâcle at Jeronimo they find their way to Brewer's Lagoon, a little settlement near the sea, the kind of village that Allie despises, because it has in his opinion all or most of the advantages of civilization, or at any rate a number of its amenities – gasoline, spark plugs, batteries, tins of food, contact with the outside world. The Foxes do not stay there, despite the invitation and indeed the urging of Haddy, their old guide. They go round to a really primitive lagoon, and here, at the onset of the rainy season, they are nearly washed away. Here Allie becomes increasingly crazed, increasingly unable to cope with the natural challenges.

This is Laguna Miskita, the dreadful last settling place of the Foxes; and it becomes the object of Allie's improving efforts. Allie is indeed ingenious, but he does not understand that the rains that are due to come will destroy his newly-planted crops, and wash away everything but the ingenious barge or boat that Allie has built as the family dwelling. In this period, Charlie sees a wild change in his father, so much so that the Zambu who comes along one day and warns of the rains to come, seems less wild than Allie himself. At Laguna Miskita, Allie creates a travesty of civilization, made out of civilization's detritus, scavenged from the beach nearby: 'fishing tackle . . . rope and rags and plastic jugs and lumps of tar, and oars and canoe paddles and cooking pots and skillets. One day we found a six-foot ladder, and on two successive days toilet seats' (299). Again it is an irony that Allie depends on these civilized amenities, as it is soon to be an irony that he is able to make his escape with his family by means of an Evinrude outboard motor.

Toward the end of the novel there is a significant increase in pace. The fourth and fifth sections of *The Mosquito Coast* are much shorter than those which have preceded, and this is as it should be because in them is compressed the outcomes, the calamitous outcomes, that are readily predictable from what has gone before. Instead, there-fore, of finding an ultimately and completely untouched civiliza-tion up the river, the Foxes find – the Spellgoods; but not until Charlie and Jerry have been savagely punished by their father for daring to wish that they were going downriver, toward the sea and civilization. When the propeller of the Evinrude is sheered and goes to the bottom, Jerry and Charlie are sent in turn to try to retrieve it; and they learn that Allie does not care enough whether they drown – he does not heed his wife's entreaties on the subject. When he himself dives and appears for a time to have perished, a sense of relief overcomes Jerry and Charlie: 'We were free' (346). But their father emerges after all.

At Guampu, the supercivilized settlement of the Spellgoods, which of course Allie wants to avoid at all costs, the boys escape for a while. It is here that they see a video-taped sermon and well-marked pathways and electric lights from a generator, and the landing strip that enables the Spellgoods to come and go in a small airplane. It is from this place, after Allie has set it alight, that the Foxes flee in the Spellgoods' Land Rover, Allie having been chained and tied by his sons. Then, wounded by a shot from the enraged Spellgood, Allie is dying – raving; and Charlie bends over him: 'Then I had to turn away, because with bared teeth I heard some-thing violent in me urging me to bite his ear off' (384). This is exactly what Polski had told Charlie of in the cautionary tale at the beginning of the narrative.

At the end of this section, Allie is devoured by vultures.

The final section is less than two pages long, and it is here that Charlie tells of the remaining members of the Fox family making their way back to La Ceiba, and home. 'The world was all right, no better or worse than we had left it – though after what Father had told us, what we saw was like splendor. It was glorious even here, in this old taxicab with the radio playing' (392).

When Allie Fox says, as he does repeatedly, 'I'm the last man', he is carrying the Crusoe enterprise well beyond its logical conclusion; Defoe's rugged individualist is assuredly a cock-of-the-walk; and his ambition, which is fulfilled, requires not tools and a knowledge of how to use them, but a faith in their efficacy. There must be an environment amenable to his will; there must be human co-operation, even with a society that countenances slave labour. I have argued that *Robinson Crusoe* ministers to our misanthropic yearnings, the end of which must be extermination for all but the hero who is the teller of the tale. So Crusoe always exempts himself: he can imagine neither failure nor extinction; his is the oblivious ideology of success, blind to the passage of time. But Allie learns to imagine failure as well as success, he who lives in the new age when the destruction of the world is all too possible. Thus he imagines, then posits, and finally believes that the USA has been blown to bits; he *wants* America to be destroyed because such annihilation will, after the fact, justify his flight to Honduras, especially because this flight has entailed certain unanticipated disillusionments from the beginning, and finally failure and death. Allie wants to be the last man not because he is confident of success – far from it – but because he wants to be the ultimate example of humanity at its most adept. In the earlier period it was possible to be buoyed by hope, even by the expectation, of success coinciding with personal ful-filment; in the 1980s, hope has become a discredited mode of feeling when attached to the economic swashbuckling that looked so promising to Defoe's hero. The hope in *The Mosquito Coast* must be contemplated apart from and in the teeth of such ambition. Hope for Theroux is a more modest entertainment.

3 The Emergent Woman

The perfection of form of *Emma* stands as a challenge, from the beginning to the end of the novel – a work of captivating arrangement and (on the heroine's part) brilliant incomprehension, concluding with the tonic chord of marriages that have been envisioned throughout, except by most of the principals; and 'perfect' is a word whose ironic fortunes trace and express the challenge throughout the novel. But more than one reader has been led astray by supposing that 'perfect' means perfect, without the slant of irony, especially at the end of the novel. Thus Miller: 'The "perfect union" of Emma and Mr. Knightley virtually *must* end the novel; otherwise it would not be a "perfect" union. It would be brought back to the state of insufficiency and lack that has characterized the novelistic movement' (5). But the perfection there sketched has already been eroded by what has led up to this comic moment. Historically, the book's fine coherence places it as powerfully indicative of the era that had just drawn to a close but to which Jane Austen's novel provides wary retrospect; the glitter is valedictory – compare *Tom Jones*. *Tom Jones* has a different kind of perfection, because its length and breadth create more space around and within it. The picaresque elements in *Tom Jones* – the journeying, the tarrying, the arriving, the episodicity of construction – prevent the sense of enclosure that is so much a part of the meaning of *Emma*. It is many miles from the spreading Somerset acres of Squires Allworthy and Western to the village of Highbury; and in those miles, in the sense of boundedness, definition, even restriction, lies a good deal of the force and meaning of *Emma*. The plot movement, from one delusive sense of awareness to another at the end of each of the three volumes, leading to the apparently full revelation that frames and illuminates the concluding pages of the novel; the deployment of characters with an entirely sure sense of movement and counter-movement, of the leading characters and their foils, of parents and their surrogates, of the clever, the foolish, the wise, and the disingenuous; all this arrangement is contained within a narration that is impeccably timed, brilliantly phrased – chapter after chapter of proper words in proper places; at every point there is what appears to be the inevitable way of expressing what needs to be expressed, of representing speech that needs to be spoken, of commenting only where necessary and always with the condensed wit that is utterly inimitable and altogether characteristic of the expression of Jane Austen.

Likewise *Tom Jones*. But the differences between *Tom Jones* and *Emma* reveal differences in which the world can be understood, in which life can be represented, in which meaning can be ascribed to actions. *Tom Jones* has its own well-defined atmosphere; the skies are distant, the meadows are generously laid out, there is room for error – even such egregious error as Tom lets himself in for. If all else fails, and if one is turned out of one's home, one can make for Bristol to go to sea. If one gets lost or diverted, one will eventually find one's way to London, where a whole world of adventures (savoury or otherwise, it does not much matter) awaits. And at the end all will come right because after all one is the son of a lady and of a gentleman, one is not without expectations (although one doesn't know it), one is handsome, and one is a young man rather than a young woman. The world conjured up by Fielding provides room to live in – amiably; and there is always the sense that there is plenty of space, including space for forgiveness: even Blifil, though deservedly reduced at the end of the novel, is relegated to a position that cannot be regarded as entirely uncomfortable.

By contrast *Emma* is by a woman and about a woman and is set in a highly-constricted world, in which, even at best, a woman is bound to behave in accordance with certain stringent rules; if these are transgressed, she is liable to severe penalties, as Emma Woodhouse learns to her vexation and also to her sorrow. But the structure never loosens, nothing comes adrift, all remains pristine. *Emma* positively glows. Jane Austen described *Pride and Prejudice* as 'too light and bright and sparkling', but the adjectives, without the adverbial indication of excess, apply with equal force to *Emma*.

Unlike Fanny Burney's most famous heroine, Evelina, Emma Woodhouse stays put; Jane Austen wants to write about what may be possible within the confines of her class and its possibilities, without the adventitious sensationalism of escape to London, which was the fate of the fortunately unfortunate Evelina. It is fair to say that Jane Austen faced the facts of a possible life rather than try to make a fantasy of fulfilment for a young lady. And lady is the word. Both Burney and Austen were interested in depicting the stratum of society from which they came; and there is much similarity between the upbringing and careers of the daughter of Dr

Burney and the daughter of the Reverend Mr George Austen, allowing for the difference in the generations into which they were born.

Truly enough, by invoking so highly-polished and completed a society, Jane Austen invites the response that Gertrude makes to Hamlet's question about the Player Queen: does Jane Austen protest too much? Just as realism is a response to the sense of a crumbling reality, so is the perfection of form of *Emma* reflective of an awareness of the disintegration of the society of which Jane Austen was a part. All her novels were written in the Age of Napoleon, and Warren Roberts' *Jane Austen and the French Revolution* particularizes her awareness of the cataclysmic events of the time she was living in; his is the most extended but by no means the only treatment of this relationship. Jane Austen did not think it was bliss in that dawn to be alive; she and Wordsworth were born five years apart. Her way of life, her style of thought, prohibited such a response. Moreover her cousin's husband was guillotined in the Terror, and she had two sailor brothers whose safety was always an anxiety to her and to the rest of her family. Temperamentally – or, to put it another way, ideologically – Jane Austen was incapable of welcoming the French Revolution, even at its first beginning; her response was to shore the props of a society that, as she reveals in *Persuasion,* she reckoned in terms of numbered days. The sense of doom that hangs over the happy ending of Jane Austen's final novel is the more convincing *because* of the happy ending. In *Emma,* however, the centre was still able to hold; and yet throughout this greatest of all Jane Austen's novels, the danger signals fly, and Mrs Elton almost has the last word. No-one has ever argued that Jane Austen wanted to jettison the old forms or that she is an apocalyptic writer; no such absurdity has been proposed, so far as I know; but I would make the point that the direction she took in the writing of her novels was toward the sense of anxiety that is so familiar to us today.

Although *Emma* by itself sets its own ironic terms, those of Jane Austen's readers who know the novels that precede it are all the more ready, no doubt, to find that *Emma* is a fable of spurious brightness, of misleading illumination. All looks to be un-shadowed and straightforward in the first sentence. There is something aggressively unqualified in the threefold claim – 'handsome, clever, and rich' – a series of adjectives that, narrative being narrative, we expect to examine as challenges forthwith.

Emma's situation and the attendant circumstances as described in the first three paragraphs of the novel are such as to make her the heroine of a dream come true. But the fourth paragraph shows the direction in which the novel is going to move: 'The real evils indeed of Emma's situation were the power of having rather too much her own way, and a disposition to think a little too well of herself; these were the disadvantages which threatened alloy to her many enjoyments. The danger, however, was at present so unperceived, that they did not by any means rank as misfortunes with her' (5–6). The crucial word here is 'unperceived' – of course. This is to be a narrative in which perception is the bridge between intelligence and success. Such is the novel's subject; such also its drift; but the reader must not think about it in general terms, generalizingly – the danger of doing so had already been demonstrated in the leakage of the epithets 'sense', 'sensibility', 'pride', and 'prejudice'. In *Emma* it is necessary to think about perception in personal and particular terms – in terms, that is, of Emma Woodhouse. Emma is intelligent and straightforward, the latter without meaning to be. Her machinations lack subtlety, to put it mildly. She deceives nobody but Harriet Smith and Mr Elton and herself; one might also add her father, but he does not form a part of her schemes. She deceives Harriet because Harriet is stupid, credulous, and adoring; Mr Elton because Emma unknowingly allows her actions to be construed as personally responsive to him, when in fact she is with improvident eagerness pressing for a courtship of Harriet by the ambitious young clergyman. Above all Emma deceives herself, and she does so because her knowledge of herself is imperfect. But Emma is not disingenuous, and she is no match for those who are; she is no match for Frank Churchill and Jane Fairfax.

So much, in a preliminary way, for the novel looked at from the inside. But it must not be forgotten that *Emma* appeared in the year following Waterloo, in Jane Austen's forty-first and penultimate year, that it is dedicated to 'His Highness, the Prince Regent . . . by His Highness's Permission', and that the words of the dedication itself also declare that the author is 'His Royal Highness's dutiful and obedient and humble servant'. As readers of Jane Austen's correspondence know, this dedication was made with more than a little reluctance. Jane Austen detested the Prince Regent and what he stood for, but his wish to have a novel by her dedicated to him made her acquiescence necessary, in the context of her own life and her own society. Her doing so forces the inference that for her this dedication is also a declaration, and with a certain ardour, even though the ardour is indubitably conventional. The gesture is there, unmistakably.

Emma was originally published in three volumes; in one-volume editions, including the Penguin edition, the chapters numbered 19–36 constitute volume II, and chapters 37–55 make up the third volume. Volume I ends after the humiliation of the Elton proposal of marriage, with Emma partially but only partially enlightened by the experience, now resolved to behave more circumspectly. At the end of chapter 17 she feels the pangs of remorse with particular application to Harriet, knowing that the young girl will be miserable and knowing too that the fault is Emma's own in having failed to discern that Mr Elton intended her rather than her protégée. It is a credit to her good nature, her natural kindliness, that she should feel stricken. But she is still so much Emma that, as she reflects, 'where the wound had been given, there must the cure be found if anywhere; and Emma felt that, till she saw her in the way of cure, there could be no true peace for herself' (143). Plain enough to all the readers of this novel is the prospect that Emma is laying the groundwork for further and deeper difficulties for herself, and perhaps for Harriet as well. 'Harriet', Marilyn Butler says, 'is a primitivist's heroine, seen with a satirical eye' (267). The first volume ends with chapter 18, with the failure of arrival of Frank Churchill; obviously, therefore, he is going to be the next object of Emma's attention.

And the second volume ends on the brink of what Emma feels will be 'an absolute declaration' of love by Frank Churchill, Emma having at first entertained the thought that he might be suitable as a replacement for Mr Elton in Harriet's affections. But shifting her view, she allows herself to be deluded once again, this time (Mr Elton shows the way) by the supposition that Churchill has been paying attention to her for the same reason that Mr Elton did.

All three volumes centre – obviously enough – on courtship, Mr Elton's in volume I, Frank Churchill's in volume II, each having a different object from what Emma supposes. In volume III there are three courtships, all of which will lead to happy endings. Thus the movement of each of the three parts of this novel is wonderfully ironical at Emma's expense, because after each of the first two she learns something important about her managerial skills. She learns that she is not so clever as she thinks she is, and that to try to arrange other people's lives is a dangerous game. By the end of the third volume, however, she learns to know herself and her own heart. She therefore deserves and obtains for her husband the one man capable of managing her. At the same time, Frank Churchill and Jane Fairfax, having learned the dangers of concealment, become more open; and so can deserve the happy fate allotted to them. Finally there is the happy ending for Harriet and her farmer, Robert Martin, which would have been accomplished very much earlier, had not Emma been so inappropriately domineering and Harriet so unsuitably pliant; Christopher Gillie speaks of Harriet's 'limp and drifting mind' (129); the polity of Highbury calls for some starch, but not too much.

The symmetry of *Emma* is too good to be true – true, that is, to life, and that is just the point. It cannot be said that *Emma* is a feminist novel; Jane Austen did not know what feminism was, but she certainly knew what it was like to be a woman in a society, a very narrow society indeed, in which the female role was conceived of as altogether passive and yielding and inferior; in which education for women was regarded as supererogatory, even in a scholarly family such as that of the Reverend George Austen; in which spinsterhood was a sentence to bounded dependency. Jane Austen's literary efforts were for ever being interrupted in the little cottage at Chawton, by the arrival of persons from the village who would come to call, and talk and talk and talk, in much the same vein as the villagers of Highbury who report the progress of the courtship of Mr Elton. Therefore, it is not necessary to be inordinately subtle to discern the sense of desperation not far beneath the placid surface of daily life among the country gentry, and especially among the women of that class, depicted in that novel, and in the other Jane Austen novels as well. And there is corroborating evidence in Jane Austen's surviving letters, where it is possible to comprehend and appreciate the Jane Austen who could make the best of her situation, who could be amused – as Emma herself is – by the ordinary daily occurrences of village life. When she wrote *Emma* Jane Austen was nearly twice the age of her heroine and she was by no means so naive as Emma Woodhouse; if she could imagine alternatives to the world in which she dwelt, she gave no evidence of such imaginings; on the contrary all the evidence points to the supposition that any alternative was unthinkable and unthought of. Jane Austen was taught to see the world in a certain way, as possessing coherence and also purpose.

To appreciate these facts is to come to understand something of the actuality of the time in which Jane Austen lived. That there were other ways of thinking as well is immediately evident when the names of such contemporaries as Wordsworth and Sir Walter Scott are mentioned. I would argue, not that Jane Austen is an anachronism – Lord David Cecil called her 'the last exquisite blossom' of the eighteenth century (115) – but that she is a transitional figure, bridging the gap between the classicism of the eighteenth century, and the romanticism of the nineteenth. The links, as we have seen, are made up of complex anxieties. By contrast, there is the utter unthinkability of a dedication by the author of *Howards End* to His Royal Highness, King George the Fifth – or, even more unthinkable, when Forster began writing the novel in 1908, to His Royal Highness, King Edward the Seventh. Within the novel itself, the Schlegel family represents the goodness of the German strain that existed in Europe at the end of the nineteenth century, but which in order to remain good had to get away from the militarism that was the inescapable portent of the time; and the British Royal Family, with their blood relationships to that of Germany, was very far from representing the German civilization of which Forster could approve. Anyway is it imaginable that a young man who came down from Cambridge at the turn of the twentieth century, intellectually nourished by the company of bright minds at King's College, a member of the Apostles, a protégé of Goldsworthy Lowes Dickinson and friend of the young Leonard Woolf, would even entertain the notion of dedicating one of his novels to a member of the Royal Family, however distinctly an intimation might be given him?

So also to be a woman and to be clever and rich, if only dubiously handsome, in the first decade of the twentieth century was profoundly different from being in the position of Emma Woodhouse a hundred years earlier. Margaret Schlegel is no Emma Woodhouse, and one of the points of comparison is that she does not need to be all three, because as an educated woman she has the resource of her own developed intellectual power to exercise on a range far different from and far wider than that of Emma. Emma's stockings are not blue, and more is the pity. Imagine the force and effectiveness of an Emma Woodhouse with a proper education. The fact that Emma is incomplete in this respect is implicit from the beginning. Margaret Schlegel is also incomplete – what makes the two women so is also what makes historical appraisal possible. Emma lacks self-knowledge of a well-defined sort; and while it may also be said that Margaret is wanting in self-knowledge, she (like her sister) is endlessly curious about herself, and she knows herself better than Emma ever does, or has to. The historical moment of *Emma* places that novel just as the historical moment of *Howards End* places Forster's novel. If *Emma* is read as belonging to a particular historical period, and it must be so read, the weight that the words of the narrator bears will be different from what it will be if the novel is set adrift from its historical surroundings.

Consider what the narrator of *Emma* says about Mrs Goddard's school:

> Mrs Goddard was the mistress of a School – not of a seminary, or an establishment, or any thing which professed, in long sentences of refined nonsense, to combine liberal acquirements with elegant morality upon new principles and new systems – and where young ladies for enormous pay might be screwed out of health and into vanity – but a real, honest, old-fashioned Boarding-school, where a reasonable quantity of accomplishments were sold at a reasonable price, and where girls might be sent to be out of the way and scramble themselves into a little education, without any danger of coming back prodigies (21–22).

Here the narrator of *Emma* appears to be firmly on the side of common sense, expressing the rough-and-ready view of the community in which such a school as Mrs Goddard's can flourish. But there are ironies here that appear at the expense of this community: the use of the verb 'screwed' suggests an application of force more brutal than the hypocrisies of such a community as Highbury might be expected to admit to; the repetition of the word 'reasonable', applying to terms that are made parallel in such a way as to propose that educational accomplishments may be purchased like goods at a counter. At the same time it is true too that these accomplishments are in a sense for sale at a school, even such a school as Mrs Goddard's, and it is implicit that these facts should be faced. That is to say, Jane Austen is writing in a society that pretends not to be materialistic though it is centrally so; the fact of buying and selling may be concealed, as Mark Schorer showed many years ago, within dead or moribund metaphors; but the fact remains. 'Without any danger of coming back prodigies' points to the sane norm to which Jane Austen can make an appeal without argument. But the repetition of the word 'reasonable' already has contained certain seeds of doubt; classically, two or more of the same do not make for more but less. Likewise, there is something suspect about the word 'prodigies'; it is larger than its context, and for that reason has ironic force, a strongly adverse representation of the particular, the eccentric, the individual.

But Jane Austen – by which here I mean the second self who is the narrator of the novel – does not always speak in the same tone of voice. Here is something that bites deeper; it is at the beginning of chapter four of the second volume: 'Human nature is so well disposed towards those who are in interesting situations, that a young person, who either marries or dies, is sure of being kindly spoken of' (181). Obviously, 'either marries or dies' is out of kilter in that it is incommensurate with the valuation that a community may be expected to place *equally* on these two outcomes. Both are important, but they do not have the same importance. However, Jane Austen makes them *grammatically* parallel, and so they give rise to the suspicion that there is a deeper intention – which, of course, there is, in the subtextual revelation that the state of the society in which marriage and death are equally interesting is disquietingly tranquil, boredom-prone, overanxious for excitement.

Setting these two passages side by side enables us to examine a paradox. The first passage seems to champion the sensible and the normal, to accept things as they are even though they are imperfect as they are; the second, to be uncomfortably revelatory – or (to put it another way) to be subversive. The connecting link between them is the ironic mastery of the first passage with that of the second; it does not take much to tip the world sideways; when it is askew, it is seen in a different and better because truer, but not necessarily prettier, light.

A third example may help to consolidate the view of *Emma* as exquisitely – and uncomfortably – ironical:

> The charming Augusta Hawkins, in addition to all the usual advantages of perfect beauty and merit, was in possession of an independent fortune, of so many thousands as would always be called ten; a point of some dignity, as well as some convenience: the story told well; he [Mr Elton] had not thrown himself away – he had gained a woman of 10,000*l.* or thereabouts; and he had gained her with such delightful rapidity – the very first hour of introduction had been so very soon followed by distinguishing

notice; the history which he had to give Mrs Cole of the rise and progress of the affair was so glorious – the steps so quick, from the accidental rencontre, to the dinner at Mr Green's, and the party at Mrs Brown's – smiles and blushes rising in importance – with consciousness and agitation richly scattered – the lady had been so easily impressed – so sweetly disposed – had in short, to use a most intelligible phrase, been so very ready to have him, that vanity and prudence were equally contented (181–82).

'Perfect' tips the balance in the first sentence; the narrator transposes the apparently straightforward account into the mode of village gossip, in which all brides – as brides – possess not merely beauty and merit as a matter of course but 'perfect beauty and merit', the overstatement providing the overbalance into a different kind of discourse, which pretends to the top of its bent, in order to transfigure the ordinariness of daily life into something less drab than the actuality. Beneath the irony one glimpses a strong sense of *boredom*, a word on which I lay emphasis because I am going to return to it. Meanwhile let it be observed that the 'three or four families in a country village' which Jane Austen declared to be 'the very thing to work on' are not shown to be contented families (*Letters* 401 [to Anna Austen, September 1814]). And the wording about Augusta Hawkins's fortune, 'so many thousands as would always be called ten', again puts the account into the realm of village rumour-mongering. 'The story told well', says the narrator, and she means among the villagers, because what they want is a fabulous re-creation of their ordinary lives, so that they themselves can participate in a realm they can imagine, or half imagine, or would like to be able to imagine, to be actual rather than feigned. Thus is Augusta Hawkins the object of what is called 'distinguishing notice', and the 'progress of the affair was so glorious' – as though this were a fairy-tale; but this is brought down to earth by the successful irony at the end of the paragraph, where Augusta Hawkins is said to be 'so very ready to have him, that vanity and prudence were equally contented'; the yoking of these two terms here being such as to make of the word 'prudence' a purely pejorative term, of Blifil-like calculatingness.

In part Emma is defined in relation to the other female characters in the novel; in part also, she defines herself by her actions, including the actions of her mind, which the narrator represents frequently. There are six other important women in *Emma*, and all by being what and who they are make their contribution to the portrait of the heroine. 'Poor Miss Taylor', as Mr Woodhouse always calls her, even after she becomes Mrs Weston, has been a surrogate-mother to Emma at a critical period in her life, after the death of Mrs Woodhouse; Mrs Weston is a mother-figure without maternal authority and without parental force, but with maternal affection for Emma. *She* is an explanation for the fact that Emma is so spoilt; the inference to be drawn is that Emma is her actual mother's daughter. Isabella Knightley, Emma's sister married to Mr Knightley's brother, is emphatically her father's daughter – a chronic invalid, full of petty fears and domestic disquiets. Harriet Smith is the ultimately simple, the malleable; because she is known to be 'the natural daughter of somebody', Emma can freely imagine a distinguished bloodline, especially because Harriet presents herself as available for the shaping, the ideal instrument of Emma's restless desire to exert her will. Miss Bates as the village old maid, is the village bore, highly respectable, and Emma has the honesty to compare herself to the woman in chapter ten, first talking of old-maidhood, then exempting herself from its pains and rigours, and finally separating herself from Miss Bates as a type: 'Never mind, Harriet, I shall not be a poor old maid' (85). As for Jane Fairfax, she is Emma's intellectual superior and even rival. She is, for instance, a better pianist. But Emma *claims* to be bored by Jane only because she always has to hear about her from Miss Bates. Actually, as she acknowledges to herself, there is both a bad and a good reason for Emma's view of Jane; the bad reason is, as Mr Knightley says, Emma 'saw in her the really accomplished young woman, which she wanted to be thought herself' (166); the good reason is Jane's reserve, openness as defined by Mr Knightley being a strongly positive value in *Emma*. Finally there is Augusta Elton, née Hawkins, who is a snob, as is also Emma; Emma would never be guilty of 'very like Maple Grove', because she is not stupidly pretentious; and Emma has a good heart, which Mrs Elton has not.

But none of her counterparts or foils explains Emma. There is a mystery about her, which can only be penetrated when we look straight at her, and meditate the challenges she offers to our efforts to understand her. In a way she is a dreadful young woman, yet it is almost impossible not to love her. She is a fearful snob, she interferes most busy-bodily in the affairs of all about her. She wants to be first in Highbury and she is first. She is truly good to her father, and although she does not like Miss Bates or Jane Fairfax as well as she should, she is never vicious. She is, on the other hand, horrid – horrid to Miss Bates at Box Hill. I am tempted to think that she represents an aspect of the psyche of her readers that is not altogether lovable, perhaps not at all lovable – but which we see in ourselves, a disposition to be unworthily impatient with the dully worthy; a desire to shine, without going to the trouble of learning how to do anything well enough (reading or drawing or playing the piano); the impulse to dominate. In this catalogue of unlovely features Emma remains lovable as perhaps her readers cannot remain lovable in such circumstances. Is that the secret of her success? Miller suggests that 'Emma's narcissism . . . is deprived of a mirror' (14); is it not rather that she herself is the mirror in which the readers of her novel see their own reflections, but in such a way as to soften the savage truths there embodied?

Certainly the movement in this novel, the development in the plot and the development of Emma's character (for these of course go hand in hand) – the movement is away from idiosyncracy and toward accommodation to Highbury's norms. There is a sense of composedness when one becomes a part of the community, as when she looks along the village street from the door of Ford's shop:

> Much could not be hoped from the traffic of even the business part of Highbury; – Mr Perry walking hastily by, Mr William Cox letting himself in at the office door, Mr Cole's carriage horses returning from exercise, or a stray letter-boy on an obstinate mule, were the liveliest objects she could presume to expect; and when her eyes fell only on the butcher with his tray, a tidy old woman travelling homewards from shop with her full basket, two curs quarrelling over a dirty bone, and a string of dawdling children round the baker's little bow-window eyeing the gingerbread, she knew she had no reason to complain, and was amused enough; quite enough still to stand at the door. A mind lively and at ease can do with seeing nothing, and can see nothing that does not answer. (233)

The *symbol* of the completeness, the harmoniousness, of community is felt by Emma herself as she goes to Donwell, on the day of the famous strawberry episode (357–58).

Will Emma and Mr Knightley live happily ever after? The answer is – yes, but. Yes, because Emma has learned what Mr Knightley has always known, that individual fulfilment comes about only within a social context, that one must subdue oneself to society's demands and commands, covert as well as explicit, if one is to achieve selfhood, wholeness, fulfilment. But when all is said and done there is a somewhat disturbing residue in this novel, and it may be another clue to its greatness. This residue is *boredom, l'ennui de la vie.* There are many boring moments in the course of the novel – not boring for us, but boring for the characters; what a terribly constricted, circumscribed, limited life is lived by all the residents of Highbury. *They* do not always see it so; but all, including Mr Knightley himself, see it so at least some of the time; Mr Knightley must bear with Miss Bates's loquacity, and he does; he must make markedly elaborate arrangements for the visit to Donwell Abbey of the various guests in the strawberry season; he must go to the ball at the Crown Inn, though he does not like to dance, and he does not want Frank Churchill to have the opportunity to court Emma. And the word 'perfect' in the concluding sentence of the novel is sufficiently overcharged to convey the sense of qualification by which Jane Austen intends the sense of eternal happiness to be considered.

For boredom appears to be a condition of life in Highbury. Accommodation to such a life is assuredly necessary and it comes about in *Emma.* But the outcome is not an ideal richness. No doubt Donwell Abbey is best served by having Emma as its eventual (though not immediate) mistress; she must await the demise of her father before that can happen. But the ordinary texture of Highbury life is perhaps nowhere more accurately represented than in the account of dinner at the Coles', an evening so excruciating that Emma is driven to make a bad and rather malicious guess as to the donor of Jane Fairfax's piano – a far-fetched guess, too, and a wrong one.

> The conversation was here interrupted. They were called on to share in the awkwardness of a rather long interval between courses, and obliged to be as formal and as orderly as the others; but when the table was again safely covered, when every corner dish was placed exactly right, and occupation and ease were generally restored, Emma said . . . [various things that ventilate her suspicions about the piano. Then:] There was no occasion to press the matter further . . . She said no more, other subjects took their turn; and the rest of the dinner passed away; the dessert succeeded, the children came in, and were talked to and

admired amid the usual rate of conversation; a few clever things said, a few downright silly, but by much the larger proportion neither the one nor the other – nothing worse than every day remarks, dull repetitions, old news, and heavy jokes. (218–19)

And consider the last words of the novel. The final paragraph of *Emma* has a great deal in it, too much for comfort, of Mrs Elton's reaction to the wedding of Mr Knightley and Emma. It also contains that word the reader has learned to suspect, the word 'perfect', to describe the prospect of happiness for Emma and her husband.

The new and more severe way of looking at the outcomes of Jane Austen's (and also other) novels is put by a person whom I am glad to claim as a former student, Rachel Brownstein. She says:

> Implicit in Austen's novels are these truths no longer universally acknowledged: that women are interesting only in the brief time they are marriageable, that marrying is the most significant action a woman can undertake, and that after she marries her story is over. . . . Married, she will concern herself with her cows' pasturage, or entertain and educate deserving relatives, and love and manage her husband and her house, and fall on rainy days upon her 'resources', her pencils and her instruments and her powers of reflection. But no matter what admirable things she does, she will never again be the focus of serious interest, a heroine. Married, she is finished. (90)

This grim view put forward by a feminist of the 1980s is more severely-worded than perhaps Jane Austen would have liked. But it is right rather than wrong. For all that Jane Austen had a happy temperament, and a large share of good luck in her short life, she was sharply aware of the limitations and frustrations of being a female of her class in her era. She repressed much – and did so more or less gladly, in order to live as satisfyingly as possible; to entertain an alternative was not a thinkable thought – for her. To rebel merely feelingly would be to act like Marianne Dashwood; to rebel stupidly would be to act like Lydia Bennet; to rebel intelligently would involve moral turpitude, as the example of Mary Crawford demonstrates. But Elizabeth Bennet and Emma Woodhouse are constant reminders that one must bridle one's spirits if one is to live well. And between the two it is hard to choose. But Emma is – perfect.

II   *HOWARDS END* AND THE DENIAL OF DOOM

Howards End is a novel of portent – facing, historically, in two directions: backwards toward an era that assumed or hoped for continuity, and forward to a war whose significance none could fully reckon half a dozen years before it erupted. The novel belongs very exactly to its decade, to the Edwardian twilight. Equally the novel exhibits the prescience that makes it recognizably a tract for more recent times. Biographically also it is important as marking the ultimate development of Forster in a direction that he was never able to take again; it is the work of a turn-of-the-century Cambridge intellectual who has retained his faith in the force of thought and in rational solutions to problems large and small. Not long after *Howards End* was published and made its impact, Forster went to India for the first time, and underwent a radical change that one is tempted to call a conversion. But during the two years of the composition of *Howards End* – 1908–1910 – Forster was experiencing certain pangs of doubt, about himself as a person, and about the shape of the world as he had learned to perceive it at Cambridge. *Howards End* still presents a coherent world whose stability is reaffirmed in its concluding lines; but there are forebodings: the dark fears of German militarism, the dregs of disillusionment at the imperialistic adventure in South Africa, together with the sense of social unrest personified in the awkwardly hopeful gestures of Leonard Bast to make his way upward.

There is another historical point to be made, on a different level; it is that before the First World War Forster was still able to regard himself as a poet. *Howards End*, he wrote to A. C. Benson shortly after the novel was published, 'is poetical rather than philosophical' – and then he went on to speak of himself somewhat self-deprecatingly as one 'having impulses of beauty' at odds with 'systematic thought' (119). that is, before 1914 he need not break out of the nineteenth-century view of the poet's role as a maker of beauty through the discovery of truths that themselves could be formed into the beautiful.

The elaborate narrative moves by which Forster takes his readers into his confidence constitute a remarkably successful effort to create an intimate circle of intellectual equals on the Cambridge model – ageless but young, well trained, agile of mind, in possession of certain common sympathies and allegiances by which the world may, after all, be saved. There is an air of simplicity because direct questioning of what has been taken for granted is – taken for granted. Indeed, the focus of *Howards End* is less on what happens to the characters than on the outcome of the repeatedly defined relationship between Forster and his audience. As a story-teller Forster is easy and informal, sympathetic, expectant, allusive, intimate. He beckons his readers to the circle that he forms. 'Certainly London fascinates', he says in one of his numerous parentheses:

> One visualizes it as a tract of quivering gray, intelligent without purpose, and excitable without love; as a spirit that has altered before it can be chronicled; as a heart that certainly beats, but with no pulsation of humanity. It lies beyond everything: Nature, with all her cruelty, comes nearer to us than do these crowds of men. A friend explains himself, the earth is explicable – from her we came, and we must return to her. But who can explain Westminster Bridge Road or Liverpool Street in the morning – the city inhaling – or the same thoroughfares in the evening – the city exhaling her exhausted air? We reach in desperation beyond the fog, beyond the very stars, the voids of the universe are ransacked to justify the monster, and stamped with a human face. London is religion's opportunity – not the decorous religion of theologians, but anthropomorphic, crude. Yes, the continuous flow would be tolerable if a man of our own sort – not anyone pompous or tearful – were caring for us up in the sky (106–07).

This might almost be the Forster of King's College lunching in hall; or, later, drinking tea in the Edwardian London in which the novel is set. And the stratagem works. The reader allows himself to become a member of the Cambridge or Bloomsbury world, despising motor cars, the cosmopolitan spirit, and imperialism; believing in personal relations, the inner life, and art. Writing, for instance, of Leonard Bast's nocturnal walk the narrator insists that 'it is an adventure for a clerk to walk for a few hours in darkness. You may laugh at him, you who have slept nights out on the veldt, with your rifle beside you and all the atmosphere of adventure pat. And you also may laugh who think adventures silly. But do not be surprised if Leonard is shy whenever he meets you, and if the Schlegels rather than Jacky hear about the dawn' (122–33). This teasing, light, ironical – and yet of course deeply serious – tone is what makes Forster unmistakably Forster, addressing not a class or a class within a class but his own kind of aristocracy, that of 'the sensitive, the considerate and the plucky' ('What I Believe', in *Two Cheers* 70). Such an audience, which appears to cut across classes and even nations, is an amalgam of Forster's own manufacture – one is tempted to say that it is the product of his hope rather than the outcome of his observation. In any event, the meaning of *Howards End* is intended to go beyond the fate of any individual character to a sense of civilization in a particular sense. It is a novel with a purpose, urgently realized, but presented with the good and democratizing manners of a young man of the upper middle class who has discovered and enlarged his intellectual boundaries at Cambridge and who would share his sense of enlightenment with others. Barbara Rosecrance is correct to say that 'the narrator seeks a relationship with the reader that both assumes and compels acceptance of his values, drawing the reader into the world not so much of his characters as of his own imaginative judgements' (15).

In *Aspects of the Novel* Forster argues that it is one of the privileges of the novelist to shift viewpoint from character to character, and he accounts it an advantage altogether. Certainly Forster as story-teller is always there, interposing even during conversations between characters. Because there is often a certain subtlety involved, it is necessary to distinguish between the mediated response of the character and the mediator's judgement delivered independently of that response. When, for instance, Helen has written to Margaret of having fallen in love with Paul Wilcox, the narrator tells of the elder sister's reaction to her aunt's objection to going down to Howards End. 'Margaret was silent. If her aunt could not see why she must go down, she was not going to tell her. She was not going to say: "I love my dear sister; I must be near her at the crisis of her life." ' To this point the narrative is conventional story telling, with little interposition by the teller, only that which is provided by the facts of third-person and past tense, and therefore removed from the immediacy of dialogue. But there follows a philosophical reflection which, however much Margaret might agree with it, is that of the narrator alone. 'The affections', he says, 'are more reticent than the passions, and their expression more subtle.' Certainly Margaret is capable of thinking in this vein, but in a highly-charged mood when she has determined on a certain course of action, she cannot be plausibly represented as relapsing here into meditative aphorism, and she is not so represented. The remainder of the paragraph is a composite of Margaret's viewpoint with that of Forster as narrator: 'If she herself should ever fall in love with a man, she, like Helen, would proclaim it from the house-tops, but as she only loved a sister she used the voiceless language of sympathy' (6).

To emphasize that he rather than any of his characters, especially Margaret, is the centre of gravity in *Howards End*, Forster takes special pains at the end of chapter two, when he comes to describe Margaret's 'strong feelings about the various railway termini' of London, and declares: 'To Margaret – I hope that it will not set the reader against her – the station of King's Cross had always suggested Infinity.' That is to say, Forster insists on his role as mediator; he takes on his own shoulders the burden of judgement: 'If you think this ridiculous, remember that it is not Margaret who is telling you about it' (9).

Indeed, the novel's opening words declare with modest insistence that the tale is to be told by a narrator who will take a direct hand in the management of the story: 'One may as well begin with Helen's letters to her sister' (compare the opening sentences of *A Passage to India*, which are written with the same kind of unpretentiousness – indeed all five of the novels bear this stamp, but in the final work, which contains the most public treatment of his themes, this presence is the more remarkable). It is the tone of a man whose 'irritating refusal to be great' is reprehended or at least regretted by Lionel Trilling, but which is a plain enough refusal, whether irritating or not (Trilling 10). *Howards End* is to be the sort of novel in which the characters play exemplary roles, exemplary, that is, of the judgements which Forster would have us arrive at with respect to the inner life, to personal relations, to affection – always as they touch a world whose centre may not hold. It is a cautionary tale told by a person who holds story-telling in low esteem: 'Yes – oh dear yes – the novel tells a story', Forster says in *Aspects of the Novel*, and wishes it were 'melody, or perception of the truth, not this low atavistic form' (17).

Trilling says that *Howards End* is about England's fate, and the claim is just (108); but Forster, ever the enemy of magniloquence, starts with the individual; what happens to the individual is of national consequence. The focus is narrow, the emphasis is always on personal relations at the expense and also in the teeth of such large questions. In 'What I Believe', Forster comes first and last to the question of friendship. While regretfully acknowledging the existence and the menace of force, he nonetheless stares it down. 'All the great creative action, all the decent human relations occur during the intervals when force has not managed to come to the front. These intervals are what matter. I want them to be as frequent and as lengthy as possible, and I call them "civilization" ' (68). Nonetheless, *Howards End* has a philosophical intention. In this sense it is didactic as well as philosophical. But to treat the major dualities of *Howards End* as I fear they are too often treated is to raise the novel to a level of abstraction to which Forster does not aspire. The unbuttoned and even sometimes languid role played by the story teller ought to forbid a reading of the book as a deployment of philosophical opposites, with the purpose of rendering a philosophic truth, distilled and ideal, or at least abstract. Therefore the proper approach to *Howards End* is through Forster's eyes as he spins the web of personal relationships that make up the novel.

The novel's epigraph – 'Only connect . . .' – is mocked by the many failures of connection in the narrative itself. Helen imagines, though only briefly, that a marriage with Paul Wilcox will be possible; her physical connection with Leonard Bast is impulsive and almost at once regretted, having been entered into out of a sense of pity and guilt. Leonard himself agrees to marry Jacky out of loyalty to a remembered affection rather than in the hope of a promising union; in his devotion he is thus a better man than Henry Wilcox, whose fleeting connection with Jacky provides a recollection in guilt and matter for repression. The marriages of Frieda Mosebach and Herr Liesecke, of Dolly Fussell and Charles Wilcox, of Evie Wilcox and Percy Cahill: these marriages mock the novel's epigraph – so much so that marriage as an institution is far from being extolled as the augury of connection in the sense called for by Forster.

There is, however, the possibility that Ruth Wilcox was happy in her marriage and the certainty that Margaret becomes so. But neither of these relationships occupies the centre of the stage, not Ruth Wilcox's, not even Margaret's. Ruth Wilcox dies in the first quarter of the book. And Margaret, the 'less charming of the sisters' (62) is – as she herself thinks – too cerebral. Her narrator agrees: 'The world would be a grey, bloodless place were it entirely composed of Miss Schlegels' (25–26). Not until the tale is told does she learn enough both to give and forgive in marriage. Truly enough, personal relations, whether marital or friendly, fail repeatedly in *Howards End* for compelling reasons ranging from the excessive self-dependence of Tibby Schlegel to Leonard's sense of estrangement from cultivated society and the Wilcox denial of the heart's reasons. Connection – and proportion – are represented by the narrator who, though he plays no part in the events that make up the action of the book, conveys a sense that civilization is possible, and that it comes into being in *Howards End* when and as he tells his tale. Forster *is* civilization. Everything depends on the narrator who, though duly modest, unites wit and intelligence, acknowledges prose and celebrates passion, clings to the truths of place, discovers proportion, and at last allows Margaret to find herself, in an outcome that is auspicious rather than tragic.

Thematically, the outer life of telegrams and anger is comprehended as making a false antithesis to the inner life of personal relations. These are the metaphoric boundaries within which the story is unfolded, and they have specifiable roots in the history of the time in which *Howards End* is laid. To put it another way, the endeavour to juxtapose them is founded in the hope that what is good and what is frightening about the world that Forster knows can somehow bring about a stronger compound. The attempt to build the rainbow bridge between prose and passion – to echo the purplest of the prose in *Howards End* – represents a hope against hope. In this novel the true harmony of prose and passion is a matter of proportion to be achieved not through acquiescence in advance, not by work and effort, but by a discovery through involvement with the land, with the rhythms of season and self. 'In these English farms, if anywhere, one might see life steadily and see it whole, group in one vision its transitoriness and its eternal youth, connect – connect without bitterness until all men are brothers' (266). It is the dream that Forster was able to entertain before the First World War, and that others – with less warrant – have been able to entertain in the more than half century that has ensued.

Such a harmony is what Ruth Wilcox stands for, and that is why her presence broods so largely over the novel, even though she herself plays so small a role in the action of the story. But the audience to which Forster addresses himself cannot be expected to divest itself of its urbanity and culture, its involvement with the panic and emptiness that are the realities of the post-Victorian world. Ruth Wilcox belongs to a past that cannot be recaptured – even in 1910, especially in 1910. The Schlegels belong to a present from which they cannot escape, and they have no clear view of the doom that will befall their class in a few short years. But the narrator can mediate between the past with respect to his present and the present with respect to the future as he can envision it; he can show his readers, as he thinks, a way to connect the prose and the passion that is not fully depicted in *Howards End*. In Forster's view we can connect by refusing to deny our sensual nature even as we rejoice in the clarities of the mind; we can connect by recollecting our indebtedness to the earth; and by being true to one another; we can connect by making judgements and forming ties based on personal trust and respect for personal freedom. Thus Ruth Wilcox: she implicates us in the connection, and Forster *tells* us about her, for the purpose of implicating us in the visionary connection that makes for hope this side of the grave.

Ruth Wilcox is set apart, larger than life, and uncomfortable in it. Such is the explanation of her failure at Margaret's cosmopolitan and talkative luncheon party:

> She was not intellectual, nor even alert, and it was odd that, all the same, she should give the idea of greatness. Margaret, zig-zagging with her friends over Thought and Art, was conscious of a personality that transcended their own and dwarfed their activities. There was no bitterness in Mrs Wilcox; there was not even criticism; she was lovable, and no ungracious or uncharitable word had passed her lips. Yet she and daily life were out of focus: one or the other must show blurred. And at lunch she seemed more out of focus than usual, and nearer the line that divides daily life from a life that may be of greater importance (73–74).

What is remarkable is that the narrator forces us to take so much on faith about Ruth Wilcox; the fact that we do so is the measure of our trust in Forster as the conductor of the piece. It is the willing suspension of disbelief. While she is alive Ruth Wilcox is a presence and a force, but she is very soon dead and thus an absence who though never forgotten is promptly supplanted. Like the house that gives the book its name, Ruth Wilcox is an emblem of continuity, of relationship to homestead and landscape. Margaret says to her sister, 'I feel that you and I and Henry are only fragments of that woman's mind. She knows everything. She is everything. She is the house, and the tree that leans over it. People have their own deaths as well as their own lives, and even if there is nothing beyond death, we shall differ in our nothingness. I cannot believe that knowledge such as hers will perish with knowledge such as mine. She knew about realities' (311). Yet even here there is the acknowledgement on Forster's part that he and his readers must live in a world where panic and emptiness constantly threaten, where the outer life pays well in many respects, and in which the motor car (representing technology's dark side) imposes its dust and stink, endlessly. At the end of the twentieth century Forster's vision of the future has limits, but the mildness of his fears did not survive even the interval to the beginning of the First World War. In any event he knew full well that the worst horrors of modernity were not contained in the symbol of the motor car but in the bitterness of social inequality and the greed that might bring on a world war. He did not envision – who did, until 1945? – the full measure of the calamitous products of twentieth-century technology, greed, sadism, and megalomania.

Within the terms of *Howards End* itself, however, there is a presentational clarity that continues to have force, even now. Thus the past for Ruth Wilcox, especially as it confers value upon place, is a touchstone, though she does not (and Forster does not) use Arnold's word. The value of the past is inarticulable, even when it can be intuited through the *genius loci,* the magic wych-elm. Ruth Wilcox represents the older view, that which can accept the fact of the past's resistance to verbalization. She shows – and in this she is fully prescient – that the intellect can fail. On the other hand, the Schlegels belong to a disputatiously rational class and age, and although they recognize that talk is not all, that the unseen is superior to the seen, they are the victims of their own penchant for words, as when they try to take up Leonard Bast.

F. R. Leavis once complained that Forster does not bring Leonard to life because he belongs to a class that Forster did not know (270). But Forster never tries to persuade the reader that Leonard is independently plausible, whatever that may involve. Granted the interposition between narrator and event, Forster's job is to persuade us that his observation is accurate, that from the viewpoint of a Cambridge intellectual Leonard can be understood as a man 'at the extreme verge of gentility'. If Leonard played a more important part in *Howards End* he would have to be judged by a different standard. And it may be a fault of the novel that his role is not more central. But so far as he is characterized in the book as Forster wrote it, the sketch is sound enough. 'We are not concerned', Forster tells us by way of introducing him, 'with the very poor. They are unthinkable, and only to be approached by the statistician or the poet. This story deals with gentlefolk, or with those who are obliged to pretend that they are gentlefolk' (43). Missing the irony here (the double-edged force of 'unthinkable', the expectation that the statistician deal altogether impersonally with the very poor, and that the poet will sentimentalize them), some readers have construed these sentences as betraying the extraordinary snobbery that is the legacy of Clapham (see for instance Stone 36). Surely they represent no wholesale declaration of contempt but an effort to draw boundaries without including within them the element of self-satisfaction. In any event, they are definitive rather than aloof, and written with the bitterness of a man who by uttering the words acknowledges the existence of what lies beyond.

Although it is tempting to read the deservedly famous account of Beethoven's Fifth Symphony as a set piece of impressionistic criticism, its role in *Howards End* is to characterize the listeners to the music in the Queen's Hall on a particular afternoon. The narrator himself is in firm control from the beginning, his own view of the Fifth Symphony being more detached and less respectful than that of any of his characters, divergent though their views are. This 'sublime noise', as the narration has it – 'such a noise is cheap at two shillings' – affects the several characters with demonstrable particularity. Mrs Munt taps surreptitiously; gentility requires such restraint. Tibby attends to the counterpoint; he is a student, and rather a pedantic student, of composition. Margaret 'can only see the music'; hers is the almost mystical apprehension, free from pictorial imagery, that – by inference – the readers of *Howards End* understand to be the best kind of listening. But Helen, who has a pictorial imagination, sees 'heroes and shipwrecks in the music's flood', and it is mainly her version, rather than that of Forster, to which the reader is treated in this chapter. It is the impulsive and passionate girl who summons up goblins stalking and elephants dancing. 'Gusts of splendour, gods and demi-gods contending with vast swords, colour and fragrance broadcast on the field of battle, magnificent victory, magnificent death! Oh, it all burst before the girl, and she even stretched out her gloved hands as if it was tangible' (31). The reminders persist: the goblin motif is a product of Helen's imagination; Beethoven's Fifth Symphony so conceived is hers and not that of Margaret or of Forster. 'The goblins were there. They could return. He [Beethoven] had said so bravely, and that is why one can trust Beethoven when he says other things' (31). Helen has already been shown to be a credible though undependable witness, in her response to the Wilcox family. She is far from mendacious, but she is unstable – a victim of her own impulses, given to extravagance and thus inaccuracy of response. It is she, not the narrator, 'who can trust Beethoven when he says other things'. To Forster, destiny and music are not thus reducible; and it is an error, an important error, to impute Helen's version to Forster, however sympathetic he may be to what she feels. (In 'The Raison d'Étre of Criticism in the Arts', Forster takes to task as idiosyncratic self-indulgence the practice of picture-making as criticism.) The fact is that Margaret and Helen and even Tibby represent aspects of Forster in *Howards End*; but the Beethoven chapter belongs more fully to Helen than to the other two – and for a reason: because Helen, in a fumbling and initially ineffectual way, is going to be able to build the rainbow bridge between prose and passion that will make the final outcome of the book a hopeful rather than a bleak prospect; her child by Leonard Bast will reclaim the house and the fields of *Howards End*.

The Fifth Symphony chapter therefore functions in a special way. The plot action turns on Helen's inadvertent removal of Leonard Bast's umbrella and his introduction to the world of Schlegels. The narrator does not say what Leonard's response to the Beethoven has been, and this reticence, despite all the talk about music on the way to the Schlegel house, brings or ought to bring the reader's judgement of the music's significance to a more moderate level than that of Helen's transfigured – which is to say, heated – imagination. Forster does use the goblin motif again, this time in his own voice, as Leonard approaches Howards End to meet his death: 'To Leonard, intent on his private sin, there came the conviction of innate goodness elsewhere. It was not the optimism which he had been taught at school. Again and again must the drums tap and the goblins stalk over the universe before joy can be purged of the superficial' (320–21). Here the narrator has appropriated Helen's way of thinking about the Beethoven to make, metaphorically, a larger statement, which here he authenticates in his own voice as a kind of lightening before Leonard's death.

But at the very beginning it is Helen whose mistaken judgement precipitates the action of the novel because of a failure to understand the premises upon which a good life can be based. She is very young, to be sure. She has just come of age when the novel opens, and it would be harsh indeed to complain, especially when she falls in love, that she should sort out the Bloomsbury values on which she has been raised, and to which she pays the lip-service not of insincerity but of incomprehension. The letters that she writes to Margaret from Howards End are transparent represent-ations of her own naiveté, not only in their candour ('I do not know what you will say: Paul and I are in love') but also in the quality of her chatter about the Wilcoxes' hay fever and Mr Wilcox's saying 'the most horrible things about women's suffrage so nicely' (3).

In a reflective passage several chapters later, Forster explains the matter, and so dissociates himself from the judgements and mis-judgements made by Helen in the Wilcox affair. 'The energy of the Wilcoxes had fascinated her', he writes (21) and it is altogether to his credit that he makes the reader understand why she should have fallen in love with Paul, and why Margaret must take the fact seriously, even though the encounter is fleeting. 'We' – English – 'do not admit that by collisions of this trivial sort the doors of heaven may be shaken open' (23). Energy – or, as it is later called, grit – is what the Schlegels feel the lack of. But Ruth Wilcox does not feel this lack; and neither, as narrator, does Forster. If the narrator of *Howards End* is invested with the authority that as a story teller he repeatedly demands, no reader can come to the conclusion that the 'proportion' toward which the book is tending is meant to be a combination of grit (Wilcox) and sloppiness (Schlegel).

To be sure, at a memorable moment Margaret says to her sister: 'The truth is that there is a great outer life that you and I have never touched – a life in which telegrams and anger count. Personal relations, that we think supreme, are not supreme there. There love means marriage settlements, death, death duties. So far I'm clear. But here my difficulty. This outer life, though obviously horrid, often seems the real one – there's grit in it. It does breed character. Do personal relations lead to sloppiness in the end?' (25) As Margaret asks this question it is rhetorical in its demand for assent; but the reader must regard the phraseology as dubious. The narrative's answer, which is to say Forster's answer, is that the Wilcoxes and what they stand for must be adversely judged, though at last forgiven; that personal relations and the faith behind them are what must be depended on and returned to; that sloppiness is the outcome of rootlessness; and that a proper life – 'hope this side of the grave' – arises from an understanding of person and place. Trilling is exactly right when he declares that 'the outer life betrays Margaret; it is the inner life which "pays" and which, in the end, takes over the outer life' (115).

To accept the argument that 'civilization' rather than any single character is the central focus of *Howards End* cannot prevent acknowledgment of the central role played by Margaret in the narrative. Of course no-one expects heroes and heroines to make correct choices; fictional narratives are about persons who make wrong choices for what appear to be good reasons. And Margaret makes a number of wrong choices, such as her decision to write a harsh letter to Ruth Wilcox, her refusal of the elder woman's invitation to spend the night at Howards End, and her brusquely dismissive note to Leonard Bast after the embarrassing meeting at Oniton Grange. But because Margaret is what she is, a Bloomsbury character herself, there is a special temptation in *Howards End* to identify her views too closely with those of Forster. This temptation exists despite his own disclaimers. And the lines are indeed drawn – for instance, when Margaret tells her aunt that Helen's 'will to be interested' in Paul Wilcox is dead, Forster urges that 'indeed Margaret was making a most questionable statement – that any emotion, any interest once vividly aroused, can wholly die' (55). Moreover the melodramatic concluding chapters of *Howards End* represent two converging plot movements. The first has to do with the outcome of the story itself. The other and more important outcome is the drawing together of Margaret and Forster. James McConkey says, correctly as it seems to me, that Margaret 'ultimately assumes' Forster's voice, but he asserts – wrongly, I think – that this role 'ultimately weakens her connection with the physical world. Thus the intended reconciliation of the physical and transcendent is imperfect and the novel fails fully to "open out" ' (9). In fact, Margaret learns through the catastrophe and its consequences what Forster has known all along, and her accretion of knowledge is what makes possible the ending on a note of hope.

Margaret allows herself to be persuaded to deceive Helen, summoned from Munich to visit Aunt Juley on what is mistakenly thought to be her death-bed. The deception comes about from a generous motive founded on love and worry – Margaret fears that her sister may have gone mad; but it is a betrayal of their love that Margaret should behave in this way. 'To "act for the best" might do Helen good, but would do herself harm, and, at the risk of disaster, she kept her colours flying a little longer' (275). Eventually prevailed on by Tibby, who has 'the student's belief in experts', Margaret acquiesces in a plot hatched by Henry to entrap Helen at Howards End, to which the Schlegels' books and furniture have been sent. But as soon as the confrontation takes place, Margaret discovers simultaneously that pregnancy is the reason for Helen's refusal to be seen, and that the deception is indeed intolerable, the confirmation of the fears she has had of falling in with Henry's plans. Here begins, then, the series of illuminations that will bring Margaret to Forster's own level of insight, sympathy, and – so to speak – grace. 'I haven't behaved worthily' (290), Margaret tells her sister at once, and Helen's silence confirms the judgement by Margaret herself. But Helen, matured by her experience of life, is far from unforgiving, and later she impulsively and affectionately suggests that the two of them spend a valedictory night at Howards End.

From this point to the end of the book is the kind of melodrama, almost operatic in its extremity of realization, for which Forster is well known or notorious, depending on the reader's ability to accept such turns of events. Within the following twenty-four hours catastrophe upsets all plans and expectations – except, to be sure, the large expectation that the book will end as a fulfilment of the prophecies that the plot movement leads toward. The large expectation is that the Wilcoxes will somehow be defeated and that the Schlegels will somehow triumph. The very texture of the book is hopeful, so much so that a happy ending is what can be expected. But, before Helen proposes that she and Margaret spend the night at Howards End, and before the fatal disruption of the following morning throws all plans askew, there comes confirmation that the continuity of life that the house represents has its counterpart in the life of the sisters:

> Explanations and appeals had failed; they had tried for a common meeting-ground, and had only made each other unhappy. And all the time their salvation was lying round them – the past sanctifying the present; the present, with wild heart-throb, declaring that there would after all be a future, with laughter and the voices of children. Helen, still smiling, came up to her sister. She said: 'It is always Meg'. They looked into each other's eyes. The inner life had paid. (296)

But this perception, though accurate and warranted in the long run, is premature. It is not entirely unexpected that Henry should demur at allowing Margaret and Helen to 'camp out', as Helen puts it, at Howards End. After all, he has shown himself to be shocked by what he regards as his sister-in-law's immorality, and he has written a note to Margaret, in schoolboy French so as not to be understood by the chauffeur, suggesting that Helen be found 'un comfortable chambre à l'hôtel'. His refusal to assent to Margaret's urgent request is, though perhaps rather less to be expected, emphatically in character. Margaret's infuriated response opens the way, as she wrongly thinks, for a permanent break between them.

Such is her crisis and it is more significant than Leonard's fatal journey to Howards End, more significant even than his death and Charles Wilcox's conviction for manslaughter; for, while the crisis portends the dissolution of her marriage, she decides to go with Helen to Munich. Because she is so sympathetically portrayed the realization of the possibility is made to seem a possible good, though in fact it would mean a spiritual and personal deracination as profound as that of Tibby, and a defeat of even greater magnitude.

For Margaret does love her husband, and this love is taken seriously in the book's terms. Helen loved Paul Wilcox briefly; the fact that she loves him no longer may be a judgement on her, though Margaret in a notable speech pleads for tolerance of changeableness or at least of change in such matters. Tibby's withdrawal from human contact is adversely criticized, but not wholly condemned; it is a possible way. Like the Wilcox men Tibby suffers from hay fever, that signal of nature's betrayal of a heart that does not love her. Nor does he love other people. Margaret, however, never stops loving Henry Wilcox, even though she has no hope of breaking his opacity. As it happens she does not have to do so; events break Henry, and when he is broken the relationship between husband and wife is resumed on a stronger basis than before. 'The humanity in Henry Wilcox', as Christopher Gillie says, 'responds to the maturity of Margaret Schlegel whose discernment crosses the barrier between them' (117).

Henry learns, his son having been convicted and imprisoned, to make the connections that Margaret has implored him to make. Superficially, no doubt, he realizes that his relationship with Jacky is not incomparable to that of Helen with Leonard: both are adulterous. Equally, the responsibility for Leonard's death must be borne on Wilcox shoulders. Henry, however incompletely, connects – and his decision to leave Howards End to Margaret demonstrates the point neatly, especially as the other members of the family, including even the lately-arrived Paul, resist so strenuously this manifestation of grief. But Margaret herself does not learn to connect until the catastrophe forces on her the knowledge of the depth of her love for her husband, the importance of the comradeship of her sister, the importance to her life of residing at Howards End.

Howards End ends triumphantly, its resonances of plot deve- lopment going beyond words to hints of what Margaret calls the unseen. 'Don't brood too much', she told her sister much earlier, 'on the superiority of the unseen to the seen. It's true, but to brood on it is mediaeval. Our business is not to contrast the two, but to reconcile them' (101–02). Not surprisingly, Forster is always ready to declare himself on the side of the poets and prophets as against what Dickens called men of fact. Near Howards End 'lay the house of a hermit – Mrs Wilcox had known him – who barred himself up, and wrote prophecies, and gave all he had to the poor. While, powdered in between, were the villas of business men, who saw life more steadily, though with the steadiness of the half-closed eye' (320). But the humanist in him after a time revives, and he looks toward the things of this world. 'Again and again must the drums tap, and the goblins stalk over the universe before joy can be purged of the superficial' (321). The train of images first imputed to the suggestible Helen on hearing the Beethoven, and now asso- ciated with Leonard as he lies dying, thus acquire a greater force. In the nightmare of events that follow on Leonard's arrival at Howards End in the early morning, Margaret comes to realize the strength and also the circumference of her faith: 'There was hope this side of the grave; there were truer relationships beyond the limits that fetter us now. As a prisoner looks up and sees stars beckoning, so she, from the turmoil and horror of those days, caught glimpses of diviner wheels' (327). But she has not yet her final illumination, not even yet. Henry's collapse opens the series of insights that figure in the last chapter of the novel, fourteen months after the events described in the immediately preceding chapters. Margaret learns, finally, the secret of forgiveness. In order to do so she learns, what she has always preached, proportion after trial and error: 'though proportion is the final secret, to espouse it at the outset is to ensure sterility' (192).

The finding at the end of the novel is affirmative – for civilization.

Forster discovers or reveals it to be fragile and perpetually endangered but, surprisingly enough, strong enough to withstand what might look to be fatal blows. Forster as narrator of the book has promised this astonishing prospect. His revelation is that intelligence is strong enough, that personal relations can endure, that culture can survive the collision with the anarchy of panic and emptiness, that love can succeed. The close of *Howards End* is idyllic, a joyous tableau, at once prophetic and fabulous: ' "The field's cut," Helen cried excitedly – "the big meadow! We've seen to the very end, and it'll be such a crop of hay as never!" ' (340). Such a vision could not long survive, and Forster knew it – indeed the novel shows that the vision must have an end. But Rose Macaulay who as a contemporary was sure enough of the ground could say in 1938 that '*Howards End* stands as a delicate and exquisitely wrought monument to an age when liberty, equality, and fraternity were not absurd cries, when the world was not in so perilously catastrophic a state that to pursue art, grace, elegance and wit savoured of lack of public spirit, when culture was something other to writers than the negation of Fascism, and intellectual liberty was a personal rather than a political aim' (126–27). True enough, and certainly well said; but the darkness before this light, especially the death of Leonard Bast so recently depicted, enforces the sense of qualification or tentativeness or temporariness or fragility that obtains here. There remains what Malcolm Bradbury calls 'the voice of irony', which is 'relevant throughout. There is a residual sense of disturbance, a sense of pervasive anarchy, which is central to this book as it is to its successor, *A Passage to India*' (143). Many years after he finished writing the book Forster was to tell directly of the importance to himself of the original of Howards End, near Stevenage. 'From the time I entered the house at the age of four, and nearly fell from its top to its bottom through a hole ascribed to the mice, I took it to my heart and hoped . . . that I should live and die there. We were out of it in ten years. The impressions received there remained and still glow . . . not always distinguishably, always inextinguishably – and have given me a slant upon society and history' (*Marianne Thornton* 301). It is this slant, corrected by maturity and modified by other experience, that makes the dominant focus of *Howards End*. It is the slant of a liberal who outlived the war that impended in 1910 and still other wars and defeats, and whose liberal spirit burns still, however faintly.

4 Anarchy and Apocalypse

I *THE SECRET AGENT:* THE BEGINNING OF THE END

To go from the world of *Howards End* to that of *The Secret Agent* is to
walk from the drawing room into the streets, from a genteel and
protected atmosphere to a world that is immediately rather than
distantly dangerous. It is to go from the ultimately resolved threat of
personal disaster to a turgidly public realm, where disintegration is
not an individual but a social possibility. To consider that these two
novels were written in the second half of the same decade, and also
that they are both laid in Edwardian London, to think of these
novels as contemporaneous is to begin to understand the gulf that
lay between the much-privileged persons that made up Bloomsbury and the emigrant Pole who made London his own, and yet
remained in an important sense an outsider. Certainly Conrad's
ability to treat persons beyond the range of Forster's experience, to
penetrate to the lower edges of the middle class and beneath, and to
make credible the actions in which these classes engage, gives a
sense of the gloomy atmosphere of a London in which the cult of
personal relations would be an unthinkable luxury. While it is just
possible to imagine Conrad's lady patron at a luncheon given by the
Schlegel sisters – perhaps the Assistant Commissioner's wife
would also be invited – it is impossible to suppose that any of the
other characters of *The Secret Agent* would be permitted to darken
the doors of the house in Wickham Place, without having lost an
umbrella in the Queen's Hall.

In the reign of Edward VII Conrad was not alone in thinking that
the structures of civility were threatened, that they were more than
threatened; and he treated the subject again and again, with special
force in *Nostromo*. After finishing that work, Conrad turned – as he
says in the Author's Note to *The Secret Agent* – to the profoundly
personal *Mirror of the Sea* (ix). This pair of facts helps to set the terms
of the insistence, in the subtitle of *The Secret Agent* and also in the
dedication, that this is a 'simple tale'. Conrad could here bring to
bear the full force of the simple root of what looked to be the worst
nightmare of the nineteenth-century liberal – it appeared to be the

end of civilization (or, to put it another way, the end of middle-class order); and the figure of the Professor in *The Secret Agent,* the ultimate anarch because stripped of or freed from the constraints imposed by belief in anything, walks with self assurance through the streets of London, because within his threadbare suit he has his hand on the india-rubber ball that will blow him and any one in the vicinity to fragments. So the subtitle means something simple in its finality. *The Secret Agent* is premonitory; in 1914 Conrad wrote of Poland that 'all the past was gone; and there was no future whatever happened; no road which did not seem to lead to moral annihilation' (*Notes on Life and Letters* 178, quoted in Watt 1979, 8). There are strong biographical reasons for Conrad's prescience, including the Polish fear of Russia; suffice it to say here that actual exile made for a sense of alienation more profound than that visited on any of his contemporaries.

By the same token Conrad is distinctly Edwardian rather than Victorian, as John Batchelor points out in an extended comparison of Conrad's beloved Dickens with Conrad himself: 'The difference from the world of Dickens or of any other mid-Victorian novelist is . . . that however "dark" Dickens's imagination became . . . his world rests on certain assumptions which remain intact: that order and honest work are good, that there is a consensus of "Christian" values, loosely defined, to which a novelist can confidently refer. Behind Conrad's work is no such consensus. A social order which has to be sustained by Heat, Vladimir and Verloc to preserve "the gorgeous perambulator of a wealthy baby being wheeled in state across the Square" is an artifice in which all classes are equally degenerate' (70). Truly enough there is a decline in social faith exhibited in the work of Conrad (as also in James); and Conrad's rejection is encompassingly nihilistic, but it is not undiscriminating; between the soft-headed patroness and the grubby-minded anarchists there is a choice, and the more civilized class is to be preferred, though hardly to be embraced as representing the ideals of a benign social structure. Yet Frank Kermode is surely right to stress the darkness of Conrad's vision in *The Secret Agent.* 'For Conrad the attempt on the Observatory where time and space are zero and the imperial city is the devourer of the world's light is all the more nihilistic in that it is carried out by an idiot at the instigation of an informer whose master is a corrupt and foolish politician' (49).

One of the ways of measuring the distance between the views of the world before the First and after the Second World Wars is to think on the boundaries of the sense of doom. Of course, Conrad feared the future that he looked toward, and *The Secret Agent* encapsulates that fear in a specific way. But it is localized; if the anarchists could be exposed for what they are, a small band of persons without an anchor in actuality, and with grievances hardly warranted at any rate, the threat could be contained, at least for the foreseeable future. The other threat, which Conrad sees so well and writes about so feelingly, is that suggested by the interlocking series of arrangements, sub-rosa agreements, illegal and extra-legal co-operations, by which the capitalist world appears to survive, and even to flourish, such that the world of policemen and the world of thieves is equally corrupt, secretive, subversive – contrapuntal and complementary, as are the Professor and Chief Inspector Heat in Conrad's novel. 'The mind and the instincts of a burglar', the narrator tells us, 'are of the same kind as the mind and the instincts of a police officer' (92). In the present, in our present, in Graham Greene, brutality is much more notoriously widespread; and the analogue in *The Human Factor* to Chief Inspector Heat is none other than Cornelius Muller, the South African policeman of sinister and brutal motive. In *The Secret Agent* the plot to blow up the Greenwich Observatory fails, and the only immediate victim of the explosion is the idiotic Stevie. Winnie Verloc remains uncorrupted herself, and her suicide at the end signalizes her radical disillusionment, but never any kind of corruption; she has nothing to be corrupt about, for in remaining loyal to her brother she has fulfilled her sense of obligation to herself as a human being, and to Stevie as well. They are the same; the loyalty costs her no betrayal. But, in *The Human Factor*, in order for Maurice Castle to be loyal to his wife and to her son, he must betray his country; ultimately he must flee to Russia and live a life of traitorous exile. Regarded from the viewpoint of the 1980s, the imagination of disaster that Conrad depicts in *The Secret Agent* appears to stop short; like all others who viewed the world before 1945, Conrad was incapable of imagining the totality of disintegration that the atomic and subsequent big bombs made all too possible. Nor was August 1945 the whole of the lesson to be so cruelly learned. The sudden illuminating flash revolutionized historical thinking, brought into focus the meaning of war and what lies behind war, including the death camps, and the disposition to cruelty and evil that no technological or intellectual progress can banish. Greene has a keen but by no means unique or even unusual sense of post-1945 doom; what makes him stand out is the pellucidity and also the sympathy with which he causes his vision to be realized.

Without resorting to the stratagem of a Marlow, Conrad here manages nonetheless to establish a strong sense of narrative definition; the narrator is self-defining in certain ways important to the intention of the narrative. While Forster's narrator is somewhat languidly self-confident, his assurance springing from indigenous security (Forster having been born to the right class at the right time and in the right place), Conrad's narrator is less ready to unbend, or rather his unbending takes place from a more formally organized sense of the self. Even Marlow, with his asides, his knowing allusions to the usual ways of doing things at sea, his wielding of his story-telling cigar, cannot be imagined as the easy inhabitant of a university senior common room, or the drawing room in Bloomsbury in which tea is taken with Bloomsbury talk. The narrator of *The Secret Agent* is unnamed and he takes no part in the action of the tale; he is detached in the sense that he distances himself and therefore also the reader from the sordid events that he describes; he is *above* the events that unfold in the narrative, and the moral implications of the altitude of telling are reinforced, even more precisely defined, by this clarifying altitude. The narrator, in making his readers view things his way, likewise and simultaneously makes the readers into an audience that will respond as Conrad wants them to respond and thus define the boundaries within which the meaning of the novel is to be found.

Thus, in the second paragraph of the first chapter, the narrator describes Verloc's dwelling as follows: 'It was one of those grimy brick houses which existed in large quantities before the era of reconstruction dawned upon London'. The narrator is speaking of the house *de haut en bas*; he is also making a critique of progress in the felicitous choice of the word 'dawned', ironically aimed at the observable development brought about by the prosperity of the times. It is a politically-charged, but somewhat vague, usage – and the narrator claps us on the shoulder, so to speak, to bring us into accord with his viewpoint on the matter. Likewise, the 'hopelessly cracked' bell at the entrance of the little sex shop that Verloc keeps is said 'at the slightest provocation' to clatter 'behind the customer with impudent virulence' (4), the distancing of the narration from the event already having been achieved by the description of the clientele in such a way as to exclude any of the persons who might reasonably be expected to be reading the account provided.

Nothing, therefore, could be further from evenhandedness or objectivity in the narrative, even though the narrator is calmly and unapologetically omniscient. When Winnie's mother is described – 'a stout, wheezy woman, with a large brown face' (6), the narrator comments: 'She considered herself to be of French descent, which might have been true' – an observation that by no means indicates his incapacity to discover the actual provenance of the old woman, but shows rather that she had pretensions of lineage needing to be exposed, whether or not her claims might on examination turn out to be true; and the exposure, such as it is, need not do more than underscore the modesty of her place in life as the widow of 'a licensed victualler of the more common sort' (6). The narrator belongs to a higher, more privileged class, and must look with a certain sense of amusement at the petty pretensions of the likes of Winnie's mother's class. Also, of Stevie: 'Under our excellent system of compulsory education he had learned to read and write' (8) – the quality of excellence collapsing under the aspect of the boy's competence as a grown-up; his ability to deal with life is seriously compromised by what he learned at school.[1] The narrator of *The Secret Agent* is on the side of achieved civilization, that is, he favours order with all its costs; and, in assuming that his readers will be of the same frame of mind as his own, he contrives to induce his readers to share his views. Thus: 'The majority of revolutionists are the enemies of discipline and fatigue' (53) is a remark that could hardly be made after 1917, except by an ignoramus, which Conrad was not. That he could put such words in the mouth of a narrator behind whom he stands morally, places the novel in its period. It also establishes the context in which the critique of anarchism is to be understood. Likewise, the following generalization: 'The way of even the most justifiable revolutions is prepared by personal impulses disguised as creeds' (81).

As always Conrad wants to offer ultimate explanation; he is stung by the teasing urge to discover and articulate the truth of things. Very possibly – indeed probably – he is so driven because in his

[1] There is an historical context for this remark by the narrator: the Education Act of 1870, which made provision for education on a sufficiently broad scale to engender further legislation ten years later that for the first time introduced compulsory education in Great Britain. The initial controversy over these measures was renewed by the passage of the Education Bill of 1902, providing for radical reforms in the organization and funding of secondary schools. See Ensor 146 et seq.

mind this ultimate shape is in doubt. In this respect he is half a late Victorian or a man of the turn of the nineteenth into the twentieth century, an heir of Matthew Arnold in having found the usual explanations wanting, but having found nothing to take the place of the expectations upon which he had been brought up. Also, there are emigration and acculturation, the mastering of a new language; these surely exacerbated the sense of rootlessness and restlessness, and lie behind the metaphysical yearnings. But they are metaphysical and to that extent still Victorian. On the other hand, as he gives a glimpse of the undecidable he can be read as belonging to the 1980s and 1990s; we know what he is talking about, though we are made less comfortable by his designation of the abyss by way of abstractions that look grandiloquent today just as they did for Beerbohm at the time – see 'The Feast by J*s*ph C*nr*d'.

Like Henry James before him and with an intensity brought about by the South African War, Conrad acknowledged a contemporary threat to order. He had the Victorian, and also the Edwardian, bifurcated sense of the future; the idea of progress collided with other ideas at least equally potent. And, like James in *The Princess Casamassima* well before the end of the century, Conrad could imagine an explosion that would bring it all down (as the anarchists hoped); he could not imagine an orderly alternative that would provide for civilized living. The anarchists whom he depicts in *The Secret Agent* are foggy-minded or nihilistic. Therefore symbolic destruction (and the Greenwich Observatory was a fine symbol) would bring about the possibility of a new beginning, a rebuilding from the ashes. Conrad, by his depiction of this motley crew, reveals not so much a profound understanding as a profound contempt. Perhaps he also shows, as does James at the same time, a fear of history itself. Nonetheless, there is in Conrad's thinking a limitation in the possibility of what is to be final: Conrad (like James) could envision a structural collapse, the end of a civility, without being able to entertain the possibility of total and irreversible destruction, the brutally commonplace entertainment on the imaginations of persons living in the closing decades of the twentieth century. George Woodcock says that 'the late 1880s and the 1890s were the real heydey of English anarchism, when its gospel spread in many directions and influenced a considerable fraction of the numerically small socialism movement' (445). And it has long been known that Conrad was better acquainted with the movement generally, and the Greenwich explosion in particular, than he acknowledges in his preface: the connection has been scouted by Norman Sherry (228,229); and there is now no doubt that Conrad was much and repeatedly preoccupied with the subject. No wonder *The Secret Agent* is so powerful: it has the force of obsession.

The germ of *The Secret Agent* was the report to Conrad by a friend of a sketchy account of the attempt to blow up the Greenwich Observatory; the friend had said to Conrad: 'Oh, that fellow was half an idiot. His sister committed suicide afterwards' (x); this was the incident in 1894 in which a Frenchman, Marcel Bourdin, died in an explosion in Greenwich Park, when the home-made bomb that he was carrying accidentally went off (Woodcock 439). There is also a second crystallizing aspect of the beginning of *The Secret Agent,* as reported by Conrad, namely in his reading in a memoir of an Assistant Commissioner of Police, of a remark by the then Home Secretary, Sir William Harcourt: 'All that's very well. But your idea of secrecy over there seems to consist of keeping the Home Secretary in the dark' (xi), the perennial complaint of a Parliamentary chief about his subordinates in the Civil Service. In *The Secret Agent* there is the uneasy relationship between Chief Inspector Heat and the Assistant Commissioner, who knows Michaelis, the ticket-of-leave anarchist, as the protégé of the patroness who is in turn a friend of the Assistant Commissioner's well-born wife.

When Conrad says that his method is to be ironic, he is only describing – with some idiosyncracy – what is always to be his method, which is founded on a scepticism about reality, together with all the stylistic devices for representing that scepticism obliquely. Irony, after all, is historically the badge of undecidability. It does not strike me as any more surprising that Conrad should choose to be ironical in treating the subject of *The Secret Agent* than that he should be so with any of the other subjects that interest him. His greatest works have as their common denominator the sense of distance between the delusions impelled by sentimental hope or self regard against the grim actualities that man dare not face squarely. Galsworthy discerned long ago that Conrad's irony – as Ian Watt approvingly reports – 'certainly comes from his sense of the endless contest between the "unethical morality of Nature" and mankind's need to impose on the natural world an imaginary order more gratifying to his pride and his laziness' (Watt 1973, 60).

At the end of the 'Author's Note', Conrad writes, with an air of finality: 'I will submit that telling Winnie Verloc's story to its anarchistic end of utter desolation, madness, and despair, and telling it as I have told it here, I have not intended to commit a gratuitous outrage on the feelings of mankind' (xv). Of course he has not, though he was stung by some of the reviews at the first issuance of the book; but the deeper disturbance here is something that Conrad does not deny; he does not deny that he fears collapse and that he senses its approach – but, as we can now see from a distance that was not vouchsafed Conrad, without the full realization that Greene is able to provide in *The Human Factor*.

The Secret Agent is Winnie Verloc's tale. Conrad says so in the 'Author's Note' published thirteen years after the first appearance of the novel in 1907. By 1920 he is moved to write an apology which denies that it is an apology, to defend himself against the 'criticism [that] would be based on the ground of sordid surroundings and the moral squalor of the tale' (vii). What Conrad says in his defence he couches negatively: 'there was no perverse intention, no secret scorn for the natural sensibilities of mankind at the bottom of my impulse' (viii). True enough; there is on the contrary the expression throughout the novel of a yearning for order, based on mutual respect and love; and indeed a presentation of such orderliness in the character of Winnie Verloc, who is explicitly not a revolutionary, not an anarchist, but a person animated by the elemental sympathy for her mother and for her brother Stevie: for them both, but especially for her brother. For Stevie, Winnie gave up her romantic attachment to the butcher's young son with good prospects. For Stevie, Winnie sacrificed a realizable prospect of happiness because she thought she had found in Verloc the lodger, just the person who would make it possible for her to see that Stevie would be looked after. Yet at bottom there is, concomitantly, the 'tragic suspicion' that 'life doesn't stand much looking into' (xiii). So far is she reduced and battered by her experience of life. But she is utterly faithful to her perceived obligations, to her familial love that she puts before personal and – as she thinks – selfish sexual gratification. Nevertheless, she would have liked to enjoy these benefits. In Conrad's scale of values, Winnie's fidelity ranks at the top; and, as Watt has pointed out, there are compelling biographical reasons for his theme of solidarity or faithfulness (Watt 1979, 358). For that reason, Winnie's suicide has moral importance as signifying the breakdown of the structure by which she had conducted her life; her brother was that structure, and when he was gone, especially as he was so by the instrumentality of the husband whom she had married to sustain it, she is morally finished.

Within the novel itself it is Stevie's drawings that perfectly symbolize the confusion and also the yearning that characterize the England at the end of Edward VII's reign, Stevie himself personifying the anguish of imbalance by his deficiency in mental endowment, much below the level of normality, of the ability to cope with the world. Still, Stevie has been to school, he is able to read and write; and he knows how to draw – circles. He does draw circles endlessly, the emblem of completeness; but he draws them in such a way as to permit these ideas of perfection to cross and criss-cross chaotically – 'innumerable circles, concentric, eccentric; a coruscating whirl of circles that by their tangled multitude of repeated curves, uniformity of form, and confusion of intersecting lines suggested a rendering of cosmic chaos, the symbolism of a mad art attempting the inconceivable' (45). Absorbed in this crazed but by no means thoughtless drawing exercise, Stevie can be roused only with difficulty. But he can be roused, he can be inspired, by a sense of injustice, physical injustice being his particular abomination, since he was physically abused by his late father.

Such a recollection makes for strength in *The Secret Agent*, the provision by the author of adequate motivation for Stevie's role in the attempt to blow up the Observatory; his keen resentment of his father's punishments is explicitly linked to the incapacity to express himself except violently when agitated. The other side of the matter, equally plausible, is Stevie's dog-like devotion to Verloc, having been encouraged thus by his own similarly devoted sister. Thus, when the anarchists talk among themselves in Verloc's shop, Stevie can overhear them and become indignant at the injustice of the world, sufficiently indignant to be susceptible of being fired with the ambition to do something about it. It is neatly worked out by Conrad that the bomb should be detonated accidentally – by Stevie's stumbling over a root as he makes his way to the Observatory, blowing himself up but doing no other damage; for Stevie is not well co-ordinated physically, and when in a state of excitement is even less so.

The story is arranged melodramatically, the non-chronological presentation delineating the causal chaos into which the world has fallen, or which is its mode of existence. The matter can be put more generally, since Conrad's method in this respect is, as Watt remarks, idiosyncratic: 'Its break with linear temporal progression in the order of the narrative ultimately reflects Conrad's sense of the fragmentary and elusive quality of individual experience' (Watt 1979, 357). The first chapter of *The Secret Agent*, to be sure, gives the background and the setting conventionally enough. The second chapter deals with the interview that Verloc has at the Embassy, in which it is proposed by Mr Vladimir, the First Secretary, that the Observatory be blown up. The third chapter is set in Verloc's shop, where the principal anarchists are introduced. However, between the end of the third chapter and the beginning of the fourth, the deed has been attempted, though the reader finds out only little by little what has actually happened. By devoting so much of the fourth chapter to the Professor, who furnished the explosives for the attempt, Conrad is able to focus intensely on this utterly anarchistic character, anarchy taken to its logical conclusion, the more starkly after the self-deceived notions of the others have already been sketched, mainly by themselves.

Such a structuring of the narrative elucidates Conrad's far from uncomplicated reaction to the crisis of the time. The Edwardian moment was dire with portent; and it was the anarchistic movement that gave some focus to the fears of those who feared, Conrad among them. He feared the anarchists as disconnected from life because cynical about it, or ignorant of it: Michaelis and the great lady who is his patron and also the patron of the Assistant Commissioner's wife; or idiotic, like Stevie. But Conrad's fears had more tangled roots, in an irregular scepticism about the society that he observed, not English society merely, but European civilization altogether; to assign cause after effect melodramatically is to raise the question of causation fundamentally. Conrad was in this sense perhaps more radical than he knew.

And Conrad sifts causes. First, there is the police mentality, personified by Chief Inspector Heat, for whom civilization consists of a network binding the forces of repression (which is how he likes to think of civilization) and the criminal classes. For Chief Inspector Heat the criminal classes, and his contacts among them, are necessary for the preservation of civilization. So when the Assistant Commissioner, Heat's superior, intermeddles in the affair of the

Greenwich Observatory, Heat is more than merely distressed, he is afraid: 'The turn this affair was taking meant the disclosure of many things – the laying waste of fields of knowledge, which, cultivated by a capable man, had a distinct value for the individual and for the society. It was sorry, sorry meddling. It would leave Michaelis unscathed; it would drag to light the Professor's home industry; disorganize the whole system of supervision; make no end of a row in the papers, which, from that point of view, appeared to him by a sudden illumination as invariably written by fools for the reading of imbeciles' (210–11).

Second, there is the critique of the upper classes, those in power who – like Michaelis's patroness – are so wealthy and well placed that they cannot imagine any threat that would affect them adversely.[2] Yet there is a certain sympathy for this class: the Home Secretary is presented with a degree of irony, but without the viciousness of caricature; the patroness herself is shown to be harmless, at least in intention – like James's Miss Birdseye in regarding herself as exempt from the consequences of the revolutionary fervour that she helps to keep alive: Conrad's patroness is a 'great lady . . . simple in her own way . . . She was not an exploiting capitalist herself; she was, as it were, above the play of economic conditions' (108). And the Assistant Commissioner, who has married into the highest circles, is presented somewhat sympathetically as having a spirit of adventure that is thwarted by his being confined to an office in the middle of London, when he yearns for the adventurous life he has had in the tropics before his marriage. Against them must be set First Secretary Vladimir, the personification of the ancien régime, the old Europe, blind and cruel in its willingness to go to any lengths to hold on to such power as it possesses. Charming and well-mannered, Vladimir displays his membership in the haute bourgeoisie by his command of Latin, which he contemptuously brings forward to cast scorn on Verloc's lack of learning. But Vladimir is a cartoon of cynical cruelty and university wit combined with manners that can be as cutting to

[2] It is important that she is no more a danger to society than the Miss Birdseye of *The Bostonians*. Hay remarks: 'Her obliviousness contains nothing lethal, as did the ignorance of Kurtz's Intended in *Heart of Darkness*. The secret evil is perfectly under control, not so much by the efficiency of the special Crimes Department (which is very human and imperfect) as by the stolid impregnability of the island empire and the obsolescence of the Russian autocracy. Mr Vladimir is caught between contempt and fear in the face of the London police (249).'

persons outside the charmed circles as they are with Verloc. In-
terestingly – and this characterization deepens the picture con-
siderably – Vladimir in his scorn is also ignorant, as even Verloc
recognizes: 'He confounded causes with effects more than was
excusable; the most distinguished propagandists with impulsive
bomb throwers; assumed organization where in the nature of
things it could not exist; spoke of the social revolutionary party one
moment as of a perfectly disciplined party, where the world of
chiefs was supreme, and at another as if it had been the loosest
association of desperate brigands that ever camped in a mountain
gorge' (30). Vladimir's wish to provide (as he terms it) 'gratuitous
blasphemy' against the god of science finds Greenwich Observatory to be a perfect target: 'Such an outrage combines the greatest
possible regard for humanity with the most alarming display of
ferocious imbecility' (34).

By contrast, all the anarchists of the tale are grotesques. Their
views, though they differ somewhat from one to another, are
shown to be ill founded, ill thought out, mainly selfish, largely
self-aggrandizing. There is nothing of the supposed generosity of
the anarchist's faith here; indeed all faith is in tatters, in so far as
there is anything positive about it. Conrad himself had contempt
for them all: 'They are not revolutionaries', he wrote to
Cunninghame Graham, 'they are Shams' (170). Verloc himself is
said to have joined the ranks of his calling out of indolence; having
come from hard-working stock, he is averse to labour of any kind.
As the keeper of a sordid little sex shop, he has what he supposes to
be a good enough blind for his secret activities, without himself
having to turn a hand to the trade; beholden to two masters,
Vladimir and Heat, he thinks of himself as a loyalist – 'to the cause
of social stability' (239). In this respect as in most others Verloc is
the opposite of the secret agent of *The Human Factor*: Maurice Castle
in that novel is a secret agent because he loves; his betrayal of his
country is founded on affection and is undertaken as a favour that
he does not regard as treasonable in any sense that can apply to his
inner self: he regards the help he gives to the man who arranged
Sarah's escape to have been personal merely; he does not attach
international importance – ever – to the information that he provides to Soviet Russia. Conrad's Michaelis has an altogether
infantile faith in anarchism as an optimistic creed; his grotesquely
fat body, bloated by fifteen years in prison, somehow emphasizes
the innocence of his eyes and the vision that he is trying to commit

to words. Karl Vundt, the old and worn-out terrorist breathes a fire that does not burn; he is no more effectual than a fangless old dog; in Conrad's splendid words, much admired by V. S. Naipaul, 'he took the part of an insolent and venomous evoker of sinister impulses which lurk in the blind envy and exasperated vanity of ignorance, in the suffering and misery of poverty, in all the hopeful and noble illusions of righteous anger, pity, and revolt' (48). Then there is the somewhat sinister Comrade Alexander Ossipon, the former medical student, younger evidently than the others, the chief writer of propaganda for the F. P. (Future of the Proletariat) movement, whose name stands out as an anagram of 'poisons'. The roseate view is counterbalanced by the utter cynicism of Ossipon: 'There is no law and no certainty. The teaching propaganda be hanged. What the people knows does not matter, were its knowledge ever so accurate. The only thing that matters to us is the emotional state of the masses. Without emotion there is no action' (50–51). There remain the Professor, and his counterpart, Chief Inspector Heat. The Professor believes in nothing except his explosives, and would, as he says to Ossipon, sell them to anyone; he hopes for nothing more and nothing less than a perfect detonator. Like Chief Inspector Heat, but from a different viewpoint, he is able to connect those who are repressed with those who repress: 'The terrorist and the policeman both come from the same basket. Revolution – legality – counter moves in the same game; forms of idleness at bottom identical. He plays his little game – so do you propagandists. But I don't play; I work fourteen hours a day and go hungry sometimes . . . . It's I who am the true propagandist' (69–70). So he says to Ossipon, and he takes with perfect indifference the news that there has been a bomb exploded in Greenwich Park. In fact, as the Professor says to Ossipon: 'You plan the future, you lose yourselves in reveries of economical systems derived from what is; whereas what's wanted is a clean sweep and a clear start for a new conception of life' (73). So much is depicted from the Professor's viewpoint. There is also the viewpoint of the narrator, representing (it is impossible to doubt) Conrad's own thinking. Of the Professor the narrator says: 'To destroy public faith in legality was the imperfect formula of his pedantic fanaticism' (81).

Through and through *The Secret Agent* are images of the mechanical, of the dehumanization of mankind, from the 'thick police constable, looking a stranger to every emotion, as if he, too, were part of inorganic nature, surging apparently out of a lamppost' (14) in the second chapter, to the final view of the entirely dehumanized Professor on the last page of the novel. The most striking, perhaps, of these images is that of the mechanical piano in the sordid bar in which Ossipon and the Professor meet – a touchstone, as C. B. Cox has insisted (83).

In the concluding paragraphs of *The Secret Agent* the Professor has the last words and the last thoughts within the tale. He is described as regarding mankind as 'an odious multitude' (311). He knows that he has the destruction of the world in his mind, as he has his hand on the india-rubber ball in his pocket. He is described as 'terrible in the simplicity of his idea, calling madness and despair to the regeneration of the world' (311). And the last words belong to the narrator, who couches his critique of the Professor in the form of a portrait, a motion picture: 'Nobody looked at him. He passed on unsuspected and deadly, like a pest in the street full of men' (311). So the novel ends on what might be called a dissonant note of hope; the pest will be pestiferous, but he cannot undertake the wholesale destruction for which he yearns: pests are eventually exterminated. Though the Professor is a danger, he will be extinguished, perhaps by his own hand, without bringing about universal destruction. In the Edwardian world a Hitler was unthinkable, and the atom bomb beyond the boundaries of the imagination.

It is a matter of moment that Greene uses an apposite quotation from Conrad as the epigraph to *The Human Factor*. The common ground is the dehumanization that is the condition of life in the necessarily corrupt societies of the twentieth century. Conrad comes fresher to the sense of cynicism than does Greene. Still there is in both novels a hope founded on the love that binds people together, rare though it is, and temporary. In *The Human Factor* there is the love of Maurice Castle for his wife and his adopted son: the hope of love is one that is doomed to be dashed, because human relationships have inconveniently consequential loyalties that are fatally at odds with the depersonalized systems to which all willy-nilly belong, and to which all owe allegiance. In *The Secret Agent* there is but one relationship that is founded on a love that is willing to make the self sacrifices that are real sacrifices, the love of Winnie Verloc for her brother, perhaps also the love she bears her mother; but the protective fervour of her love for her brother is the stronger, if only because Stevie requires protection in ways that their mother does not. Ian Watt argues, correctly as it seems to me, that 'fidelity is the supreme value in Conrad's ethic, but it is always menaced and often defeated or betrayed' (Watt 1979, 6). By such reckoning, Winnie Verloc must be considered quintessentially Conradian. But in *The Secret Agent* there is a confidence that, in *The Human Factor*, no-one – least of all Greene – enjoys; Conrad is indeed fearful of the future; but he cannot believe in the *intelligence* of those who would destroy civilization as he recognized it, despite the uncertainties that he lived through. With Winnie Verloc Conrad could feel that life didn't bear much looking into; certainly *The Secret Agent* discloses a fear that the centre might possibly not hold. But the terms became different for the generation to which Greene belongs. Greene appears to regard the centre as nonexistent. To be sure, Conrad's confidence was fading when he wrote his important essay, 'Autocracy and War', (1905): 'Civilization', he wrote there, 'has done its little best by our sensibilities for whose growth it is responsible. It has managed to remove the sights and sounds of the battlefields away from our doorsteps. But it cannot be expected to achieve the feat always and under every variety of circumstance. Some day it must fail, and we shall have then a wealth of appallingly unpleasant sensations brought home to us with painful intimacy' (110). But to see so far is not to see the end of everything, the commonplace vision of the present day.

II   *THE HUMAN FACTOR* AND HOPE WITHOUT HOPE

The exactness of the connection – and the measure of the distance – between *The Human Factor* and *The Secret Agent* is to be found in the epigraph to Greene's novel – from Conrad's *Victory*: 'I only know that he who forms a tie is lost. The germ of corruption has entered into his soul.' In Conrad's novel these words are spoken by Axel Heyst in response to a question put by Lena, the woman whom he has rescued and whom he loves – her words and his relate not only to the subject under immediate discussion, but also and more particularly to their own relationship. Lena asks:

> 'You saved a man for fun – is that what you mean? Just for fun?'
> 'Why this tone of suspicion?' remonstrated Heyst. 'I suppose the sight of this particular distress was disagreeable to me. What you call fun came afterwards, when it dawned on me that I was for him a walking, breathing, incarnate proof of the efficacy of

prayer. I was a little fascinated by it – and then, could I have argued with him? You don't argue against such evidence, and besides it would have looked as if I had wanted to claim all the merit. Already his gratitude was simply frightful. Funny position, wasn't it? The boredom came later, when we lived together on board his ship. I had in a moment of inadvertence created for myself a tie. How to define it precisely I don't know. One gets attached in a way to people one has done something for. But is that friendship? I am not sure what it was. I only know that he who forms a tie is lost. The germ of corruption has entered into his soul.'

Heyst's tone was light, with the flavour of playfulness which seasoned all his speeches and seemed to be of the very essence of his thoughts. The girl he had come across, of whom he had possessed himself, to whose presence he was not yet accustomed, with whom he did not yet know how to live; that human being, so near and still so strange, gave him a greater sense of his own reality than he had ever known in all his life. (199–200)

Heyst has thus issued a warning, to Lena and also to himself: to form a tie is to make a commitment that is bound to draw the participants into a circle larger than and at odds with the relationship itself. The words from *Victory* used by Greene are Heyst's, and Heyst is a tragic character in his supposition of detachment; his final recognition consists in knowing that to be human is to form ties, willy-nilly. In a prefatory note Conrad speaks of Heyst's 'fine detachment [owing to which he] lost the habit of asserting himself'. Conrad, unlike Greene, sets himself at a distance from his central character.

The human factor in both *The Secret Agent* and *The Human Factor* is a tie that alleviates, even redeems, the bleakness. The love of Winnie Verloc for her brother Stevie is compelling but not so informed as Maurice Castle's for his wife Sarah. Until the aftermath of Stevie's death, Winnie does not know the dangers, contingent and otherwise, to which she is exposed in her love; worse, she puts her faith in her husband, and it is this faith which leads her to try to bring Verloc and Stevie closer together. She even succeeds in her effort, which has fatal consequence. By contrast, Castle knows from the beginning the hazard of the relationship that he has formed with Sarah, that it bears a more than possibly fatal burden; he deeply fears the outcome.[3] Even when he hopes, he recognizes the almost certain futility of doing so. His fear is well founded. For he has had to turn traitor in order to escape South Africa with the black woman who becomes his wife. Nor is there any question of his willingness to pay the price of this public betrayal privately undertaken for wholly personal reasons. The treason is that of a man who values the private life more highly than the public life; the private life is what matters; the public life is the corrupt series of obligations created by the apparatus of the state.

Of Castle's betrayal there is another aspect that only deepens the tragic irony of the whole; the secrets that he causes to be conveyed to Soviet Russia are – harmless. Castle regards his job as a member of MI6 as nugatory in the extreme, but even he does not realize until the end of the narrative, when he is safely despatched to Moscow, that he has been a pawn in a different game: he has been a dupe of his Russian masters. Not that this new knowledge makes a difference to his general supposition about the workings of statecraft in his total picture of existence: Winnie Verloc is of the opinion that life doesn't bear much looking into. Castle has been able to bear to look; he is horrified by what he sees, but as he is thoughtful rather than instinctual in his reactions, his story carries a different significance. But of all the characters in *The Secret Agent* only Winnie can be compared to Castle; Verloc, a moral nullity, is Castle's vocational counterpart in Conrad's novel, and so the distance between the two novels is, in this respect, immense.

But to move from *The Secret Agent* to *The Human Factor*, from the Edwardian twilight to the overbrilliant sense of possibly total doom of the era of the Bomb, is to be exposed to historical moments so different in feeling as to make for the sharpest of contrasts. At the end of *The Secret Agent* the Professor walks confidently along the

---

[3] John Spurling writes: 'The "human factor" of the title is, of course, Castle's own hostage to fortune, his love for his wife and son, but . . . it is not the only factor.' The other is 'to be found in darkness, secrecy and loneliness' – the death wish itself (Spurling 69–70). But it seems to me that such imaginings are the fearful side of his love for Sarah rather than a separate and alternative sense. Castle 'had learned during the last year in South Africa the age-old lesson that fear and love are indivisible' (126); this seems to put the matter as it needs to be put. Spurling, however, quotes from the end of the following chapter, in which – wakeful in the night – Castle thinks of 'that long underground stream which bore him on toward the interior of the dark continent where he hoped that he might find a permanent home, in a city where he could be accepted as a citizen, as a citizen without any pledge of faith, not the City of God or Marx, but the city called Peace of Mind' (Spurling 70, Greene 134). Again, the fear seems to me to be connected with rather than separate from the love for Sarah.

street, dreaming of total destruction, unsuspected by any of the members of the crowd that he is among. As he is 'like a pest' he is, outside the purview, outside the imagining, of the rest of mankind. But all or nearly all the characters of *The Human Factor* realize that total destruction is no madman's dream, but the stuff of all-too-normal nightmares.

In *Ways of Escape* Greene tells of his 'ambition after the war . . . to write a novel of espionage free from the conventional violence, which has not, in spite of James Bond, been a feature of the British Secret Service. I wanted to present the Service un-romantically as a way of life, men going daily to their office to earn their pensions' (296). And the novel begins just as though it were to be what Greene at first envisioned; Maurice Castle is a man of habit – he always lunches in the same public house behind St James's Street; he has worked at the same job, in MI6, for thirty years; he is a steady husband and an attentive and loving father to the black child of his black wife, though he is not the biological father of the child; he is methodical; he is punctual; he is tidy-minded. He is also, though the fact is slow to emerge in its definiteness, a secret agent; and it is worth while observing that whereas Verloc is what he is explicitly out of a kind of lazy amorality, a man who comes to regard his job as an occupation merely, without consequences, Castle is conscious of what he is doing. Though he is deeply cynical about high-level governmental arrangements, regarding all governments and systems as much the same in their consequences, even much the same in their disposition to mendacity, to venality, to cor-ruption, Castle knows that there may be a certain weight in the secrets he is passing along to the Russians, revealing for instance the intentions of the Chinese in world affairs; and, more omin-ously, the collaborative venture involving Great Britain, the USA, and South Africa, in which the deployment of atomic weapons is central. Not that Castle, with his imagination of disaster, supposes that the revelation of these secrets will make an ultimate difference to the outcome of affairs generally; for Castle, the outlook is dismal, and (like Verloc) he regards himself as a cog, an unimportant cog, in a machine which has little or nothing to do with the actual decisions made by the great powers in which the future of the world will be discovered. Verloc has the myopia of the unimaginative immoral-ist; Castle is prescient. Castle is a Greene hero, and it is not to be expected that the story that unfolds will simply be an elaboration of the daily life of a man in the Service. In *Ways of Escape* Greene goes on to say: 'The novel at last was written . . . but that did not mean it had to be published. . . . I am never satisfied with a novel, but I was more than unusually dissatisifed with this one. I had betrayed my purpose. There *was* violence – the death of Davis – and Doctor Percival was hardly a typical figure of the British Secret Service. It wasn't as realistic a picture as I had intended, and the novel was saved only by the human factor of the title. As a love-story – a married love story of an elderly man – I think it may have succeeded' (299).

Early in the novel a connection is made between Castle and Lourenço Marques, to which Castle and Sarah escaped from Pretoria. The connection is, to the reader, mysterious, even though a few facts emerge at once: that Sarah's son Sam is not Castle's son; and that Castle loves Sam for a desperate or a despairing reason, which he does not omit to reveal to Sarah when she asks him whether he isn't sorry that the two of them haven't made a child. He says he would not like to have been a father. When she asks why not, he says: 'I love Sam because he's yours. Because he's not mine. Because I don't have to see anything of myself there when I look at him. I see only something of you. I don't want to go on and on forever. I want the buck to stop here' (29).

Although it can be said that Castle is in a certain sense déclassé – having married a black, and having in other ways cut himself off from the upper-middle-class network to which his background and education have entitled him, it is equally true that in another sense his being the son of a well-to-do physician of Berkhamsted, his having attended a good-enough public school at which he was properly miserable, and his having taken an Oxford degree at Christ Church, makes him belong to the world of the Establishment. And it is made clear at the beginning of the novel that Castle is above suspicion in large part because of his background, which includes even a cousin who got a First in Greats, and is in the Treasury. But Castle's somewhat desperately dashing colleague Arthur Davis in his section of MI6 is outside the charmed circle of Oxbridge – he is a Reading man – consequently the more readily suspect in the leak that has taken place in his department. Of such flimsy materials are the edifices of trust, and also distrust, built; the indictment of the Old Boy Network, is notoriously verifiable in the actualities of the post-war discoveries about Burgess, Maclean, Philby, and Blunt. The last words of the first chapter of *The Human Factor* refer specifically to the exempt status that Castle enjoys, in comparison to Davis: as Castle says, 'Colonel Daintry wasn't very difficult . . . He knew a cousin of mine at Corpus. That sort of thing makes a difference' (24).

The utter regularity and normality of Castle's life is a matter of emphasis: the commuter's train at the same time every evening from Euston to Berkhamsted, the bicycle left in charge of the ticket collector, the childhood memories of the town (so that, for instance, he knows the geography of the Common, including the location of the trenches dug during the First World War), the modest and unprepossessing semi-detached house, with a stained-glass window over the front door depicting the Laughing Cavalier. He is so much a man of habit that when he arrives home and finds that the whisky bottle has not been put on the side board as usual, he is disturbed; any alteration in routine is a portent: 'He had always, since they came, felt certain that one day a doom would catch up with them, and he knew that when that happened he must not be betrayed by panic: he must leave quickly, without an attempt to pick up any broken piece of their life together.' He knows that he will be found out, and that when he is, he must abandon his beloved wife and her beloved son and – go the way of other defectors: 'Those that are in Judea must take refuge in the mountains . . .' (21) – the phrase runs in Castle's head; and the reader is soon able to translate the terms into those that fit Castle's plight.

But, for all the world like Verloc in *The Secret Agent,* Castle keeps his wife Sarah in the dark about the nature of his activities. She does not know what he is, though she had helped him in Africa with his intelligence work. She does realize that he is a single agent but not that he is a double agent. She does not know that he has turned in this direction as the price of being able to escape from South Africa with her. He does not tell her of the uses to which he puts *Clarissa Harlowe* and *War and Peace*; he does not tell her that the telephone calls that he receives from someone who rings off, are part of a signalling system used by his Russian contact. Sarah is fearful – but she cannot pin her fears to anything specific, even a suspicion of what he is up to, any more than can Winnie Verloc. She does, however, know that Castle will have two large glasses of whisky before dinner, too much whisky; his excessive drinking is secretive, not that she makes anything very special of that either, except that she thinks too much drink is bad for his health.

It is significant that the murder of Arthur Davis should be considered, decided on, and formulated as a plan in a country-house atmosphere. Sir John Hargreaves has a house that fits his title, his position, and his indubitably rich American wife. There is a shooting-party. There are guests called Dodo and Harry and Buffy. All the more normal, therefore, and all the more disturbingly portentous, is the meeting in this Establishment establishment to discuss the elimination of Davis as the most likely spy in the section of M16 in which the leak has been discovered. As publicity would adversely affect the relationship between England and the USA, (which would suspect England of not being able to keep its intelligence work uncontaminated), the death of Davis must be made to look natural, in order to prevent an inquest. It is an irony to the reader that the person to propose to kill Davis is – Sir John Hargreaves himself; even the Establishment has become so deeply corrupted by the corruptions of the present day, that from the mouth of the likes of Sir John himself can come such a proposal for executive murder.

This deepens the grim picture drawn by Greene of the England of the 1970s, still managed by the likes of Sir John Hargreaves, the Chief of Castle's service, a man of somewhat tattered but authentic romanticism, who likes to remember the Africa of his youth; he too had fallen in love not only with Africa but with at least one black African woman. He has kept a photograph of a black friend. Sir John has a sense of honour of sorts, the sense of public-school fair-mindedness that makes his participation in the death of Davis all the more appalling.

Percival, the classical rightist, shows how to act in the world of superpowers; he gives an oblique lesson to the good Colonel Daintry on the method of comporting oneself in the modern world without suffering the pangs of doubt and remorse; the lesson (by way of an examination of a picture by Ben Nicholson) is to confine oneself to such a small area of action that the consequences will be obscured, even from oneself: ' "Take a look at that Nicholson. Such a clever balance. Squares of different colour. And yet living so happily together. No clash. The man has a wonderful eye. Change just one of the colours – even the size of the square, and it would be no good at all." Percival pointed at a yellow square. "That's your section 6. That's your square from now on. You don't need to worry about the blue and the red. All you have to do is pinpoint our man and then tell me. You've no responsibility for what happens in the blue or red squares. In fact not even the yellow. You just report. No bad conscience. No guilt" ' (46).

When Daintry makes the obvious objection: 'An action has nothing to do with its consequences. Is that what you're telling me?', Percival gives the following reply: 'The consequences are decided elsewhere.' But, knowing that this will not satisfy Daintry, he then lies to him; he says that that if there's a criminal he will not be put to death, but 'handed over to the police in quite the conservative way' (46). Whether Daintry can believe this falsehood is not made altogether clear, but the reader is surely intended to be shocked by the straightforwardness of the mendacity.

Not until halfway through *The Human Factor* are Castle's motivations fully set forth – fully enough, that is, for the reader to understand why he became a double agent. As the narrative develops, the reader learns that Castle has not become so out of conviction that the Soviets are right and the West is wrong; he is not a Marxist, he is not a Party member – so he confesses to his Control, a man named Boris, in a memorable exchange at a safe house at Watford: 'I don't have any trust in Marx or Lenin any more than I have in Saint Paul, but haven't I the right to be grateful?' (141).[4] Castle regards his position in life as somewhat like that of the squares in the Ben Nicholson picture; although he has not looked at that picture at the house of Sir John Hargreaves, there is an analogue in that he feels himself cast by fate into a circumscribed square, meaningless in that he does not grasp its meaning, though as Percival has pointed out to Daintry, if you altered the arrangement of the squares or the colours in the Nicholson the harmony of the whole would be destroyed.

But Castle has turned double agent out of gratitude to a man called Carson, who was subsequently put to death by BOSS, the South African police apparatus, because Carson made possible the escape of Sarah; Carson is responsible for the happiness, such as it is, of the seven years since the escape. The alternative would have been the imprisonment of Sarah, whom Cornelius Muller of BOSS had thought they had trapped; Castle could thus have been blackmailed into assisting BOSS. But Carson helped Sarah, and asked in return the favour of Castle's help for Boris; the bargain was obviously one that Castle took to be fair, a personal favour for a personal favour, but without concomitant conversion to the Soviet faith.

On the other hand there is a strongly anti-British, anti-American,

---

[4] The contrast with Percival is pointed here. Percival says, in another context, 'I don't pretend to be an enthusiast for God or Marx. Beware of people who believe' (215).

anti-South African element in Castle's thinking. The focus of this dislike, or its outward and visible sign, is the operation that is called Uncle Remus, a series of agreements between Great Britain, the USA, and South Africa, for the purpose of 'defence' of their interests by way of the deployment of nuclear weapons. There is a devastatingly understated verdict on the clean-cut American soldiers incinerating the Vietnamese with napalm. Here as elsewhere is indignation on Greene's part, as he presents his views on imperialistic aims, which he associates more closely with the USA than with the other western powers – inevitably enough. Neither, however, does Greene adore Soviet imperialism. But he is less forgiving of the liberalism and fair-mindedness of the west, so cruelly betrayed by its own opacity, so readily trapped into fatal hypocrisies. Greene feels keenly the loss of the hopes that liberals were able to enjoy in England up to the aftermath of the First World War. This view marks him as a postwar figure, and there is a remarkable consistency in his outraged sense of disillusionment throughout his work. So *The Human Factor* makes a political statement (and, it must be said, a religious statement as well); to turn from the twilight of capitalism at a time when darkness impends, constitutes a political judgement in that it not only permits but invites political action of the sort that Castle altogether willingly engages in; though he is frightened, and correct to be so, by the action of providing state secrets to the Soviet Union, he does not hesitate to decide on this course. By the same token, his incapacity to become a believer of the sort that would be necessary were he to join the Communist Party, such an incapacity is politically consequential in that it prevents him from participating in the efforts of the Party to realize its goals. As a political animal Castle is a loner because such is his temper, and he must pay the price of that loneliness in that he is bound to a career of fatal ineffectuality. Not that he is entirely negative in the decisions that he takes; after all he provides information to the Russians for two immediate reasons that are strongly positive: gratitude (to Carson) and love (for Sarah). In politics, Castle's is the desperate faith in two or three gathered together who can defy, though not with ultimate success, the larger apparatus of statecraft. Such a stance forms a contrast to that of the nihilistic Doctor Percival and to that of the utterly disillusioned Hargreaves. For Castle politics begins and ends with the human factor, with the ties that people form with one another. By contrast, Percival has no ties and those of Hargreaves are in the past, in Africa. Sarah says to Castle, after she has learned what he has done for her: 'We have our own country. You and I and Sam. You've never betrayed that country, Maurice' (238). But the lesson of the Nicholson painting superimposes itself even here: Castle resembles Percival more nearly than he supposes.

For one of Greene's greatest concerns appears to be what might be called the fascistic side of the Establishment in Great Britain, represented in its ruthlessness by Doctor Percival, and in its languid but still dangerous form by Sir John Hargreaves. The reader of *The Human Factor* may at first wonder whether Greene is not having the sentimental past, represented by Sir John, both ways. At the Reform Club, Percival and Sir John expose their views a little, Percival saying of his being a member of the Club: 'You must know that to be a member here I had to sign a declaration in favour of the Reform Act of 1866. True, that Act was not so bad as some of its successors, like giving the vote at eighteen, but it opened the gates to the pernicious doctrine of one man one vote. Even the Russians subscribe to that now for propaganda purposes, but they are clever enough to make sure that the things they can vote for in their own country are of no importance at all' (98). So speaks Percival, to which Hargreaves replies: 'What a reactionary you are, Emmanuel' – and then he goes on to discuss the possible superiority of steak-and-kidney pudding to steak-and-kidney pie. The juxtaposition shows two things, the incapacity of Hargreaves to argue the matter of Percival's political views, or his unwillingness to do so; and his comfortable, or more or less comfortable, supposition that despite all the changes that have taken place in the ways of thinking about the way the world looks since Rider Haggard's day, it will somehow go on, that it will continue to provide the substantial provender of the Reform Club, that the club itself will continue to exist as well, safely assimilated. Thus is the possibility of a sentimental portrait of Sir John thoroughly effaced.

Against these two men is the ineffectual Daintry, who lives by himself in a flat above Overton's restaurant in St James's Street. He has a former wife who scorns him and a daughter whom he loves but whose way of life is so different from his own that he can hardly do more than wonder at the gap between them, and try to close it. There is some good comedy when father and daughter dine together at Stone's, where she tells him about her forthcoming marriage. In this encounter Daintry is presented sympathetically as embodying commendably comprehensible values. They are old-fashioned values, and how far should the reader go in associating these with Greene himself? Perhaps too far. Perhaps this is where Greene is dangerously sentimental, dangerously, that is, to the consistency of his critique.

Another viewpoint is provided in the picnic enjoyed by Castle, Sarah, her son Sam, and Davis. The latter proves to be a winning companion, adept at hide-and-seek, which Sam much likes. But while Castle and Davis are by themselves in a hiding place, Davis confides his fears of being watched and followed. There is something sadly engaging in the idyllic quality of the picnic and its surroundings, even though it fits only with difficulty the picture that Greene is drawing in *The Human Factor*. Here is to be observed a vein of primitivism, the sense that only in the most regressive circumstances and rituals is to be found authenticity. With shocking consistency Greene dares to expose this view elsewhere; at the meeting at his house with Cornelius Muller, Castle regards the African with less fear than his bullying subordinate officer: 'Captain Van Donck was a brutal and simple man who believed in something, however repugnant – he was one of those one could forgive. What Castle could never bring himself to forgive was this smooth educated officer of BOSS. It was men of this kind – men with the education to know what they were about – that made a hell in heaven's despite. He thought of what his Communist friend Carson had so often said to him – "Our worst enemies are not the ignorant and the simple, however cruel, our worst enemies are the intelligent and the corrupt" ' (124). To put together these two episodes is to see in Greene a primitivism as wary, conscious, and sophisticated as that sketched by Rousseau himself.

Although Castle sees himself as a man without faith, he is presented differently by the narrator and thus perceived differently by the reader. So, although there is a close association between the Greene who narrates and the hero of *The Human Factor* – so close an association as to grant Castle a special authority comparable to that granted Marlow by Conrad – there is a parting of the ways in the matter of religion; association and identity part, discernibly and definitely, when Castle goes to report at Watford to Boris, his Control in the Soviet spy network. Boris, as Castle observes, is the nearest thing Castle has to a priest – 'a man who received one's confession whatever it might be without emotion' (148). That is, Castle recognizes something of the function that he is performing. So much is clear enough; yet Castle places himself beyond the pale of the possibility of confession, because he regards himself as beyond the possibility of faith. But that such an analogy should occur to him is a signal of Greene's intention to connect Castle to religious imperative. Again, when Castle goes to Watford in a vain effort to find Boris and to confess to him, he takes refuge in a hideous modern Catholic church, where he is turned away by the priest at the confessional box after having admitted that he is no Catholic; but here, and the reader sees it clearly though Castle does not, the repellent scene and the irritated denial provide a sketch of a debased church rather than the absence of a God; Castle apprehends the first but cannot connect with the second, strongly impelled though he has been.

Then there is the Ben Nicholson figure of speech without the Nicholson allusion. In his interview with Castle, Boris says. ' "We live in boxes and it's they who choose the box." How often he had heard that comparison in his own office. Each side shares the same clichés' (149). The repetition of this motif sketches itself into something larger, into Greene's vision of wholeness that has been little altered in the years of his maturity – a vision of wholeness based on the small unit of love and child-bearing, on the family, a repetition of the family life he had as a headmaster's son in Berkhamsted. Greene appears to be driven, as are so many others of the mid- and later twentieth century to a view in which personal relations, even familial relations, are to be accounted the relevant unit; a kind of view also of a more advanced sort, in which heroism and villainy can be clearly demarcated and differentiated one from the other – thus the allusion to Rider Haggard. There is also Castle's reading of *Robinson Crusoe* when he has gone to Moscow. What appears to appeal to Castle in Defoe's novel is the simplicity of the differentiations that Crusoe is able to make. It is not Crusoe's exile to a desert island that Castle finds comparable to the exile of himself to Moscow, but the straightforwardness of the list of advantages and disadvantages of his position, which Crusoe is able to set out in two columns, with a balancing of the one against the other, item by item. In Moscow, at the end of his journey, Castle observes these balancing columns. 'Well,' he reflects, 'he had the green wicker armchair, the gravy-stained table, the uncomfortable sofa, and the stove which warmed him now. They would have been sufficient if Sarah had been there' (318) – and herein lies the big difference between Castle and Robinson Crusoe, for Crusoe needs no-one, and Castle needs his Sarah. But it is not the only difference.

Although Castle has a neat desk and is a list maker – and is disturbed when he finds that the bottle of J&B whisky has not been put for him in its accustomed place, his propensity also marks a contrast. For Crusoe the making of the lists and the reckoning up are significant of something substantial and true. They mean something. They *are* reality. But for Castle such tidiness is the mere apparatus of despair against the perceived chaos.

For the most part, the narrative is presented from Castle's viewpoint with the exactness of sardonic reflection, ascribing the thoughts intimately and closely to Castle without the interposition of an intermediary; that is, the third-person narrative takes on itself the power of ascribing these thoughts convincingly, without any intermediate irony. On the other hand there are important scenes in *The Human Factor* that take place away from Castle, episodes in which he takes no part, scenes from which he is absent and from which he would be excluded if necessary. Among these are the chapters laid in Sir John Hargreaves' country house and others laid at the Reform Club and the Travellers Club, where Hargreaves and Percival meet for lunch to discuss Davis's possible defection and what to do about it. Moreover, in Part five, the narrator gives a generous account of Sir John Hargreaves's sense of Africa, his romantic sense of a colonial past in which he has had a part; here also the narrator's private account – in the sense that it is a representation of Hargreaves's unshared responses – to a reading of *The Way We Live Now*. By the revelation of the ways of the workings of Sir John's mind, the narrator is able to draw an analogy between him and Castle, both being willing to go to extremes of sorts to achieve their ends, Castle to repay the debt incurred when his friend Carson helped with the escape of Sarah from Pretoria, Hargreaves to countenance the death of Davis in a desperate effort to bring back a way of life that time has overtaken. Thus in reading the Trollope novel, he feels drawn to Melmotte of all people, the discredited central figure; there is a sense of wonder on Sir John's part at the audacity – the word is Trollope's – of Melmotte's taking his dinner in the dining room of the House of Commons after he has been disgraced. The reason is that Melmotte, shunned by his colleagues in the House of Commons, is isolated in a way that Hargreaves feels himself to be isolated in the world of new politics, the world of a different Africa, the world of Uncle Remus; in the event Hargreaves feels sympathy, even friendship, for Melmotte.

But when Castle encodes what he then thinks is to be his final report, against a passage from *War and Peace*: ' "You say: I am not free. But I have lifted my hand and let it fall." It was as if, in choosing that passage, he were transmitting a signal of defiance to both the services. The last word of the message, when it was decoded by Boris or another, would read "goodbye" ' (187). The irony of this message will be fully exhibited when a further message is transmitted to Moscow. Castle is not free; he is never to be free of the consequences of human involvement. And that is the larger, indeed the largest, exhibition of *The Human Factor*. Castle himself comes to this realization at that later time: 'The last encoded report with the final word "goodbye" had been premature and the passage he had chosen, "I have lifted my hand and let it fall", was no mark of freedom in the world of Uncle Remus' (224). This passage indicates the distance between the world as conceived by the man who wrote *The Secret Agent* and the man who wrote *The Human Factor*.

For this new world, the world of the aftermath of the First World War, exhibits the debasement of the idea of the sanctity of personal relations. In the second half of the 1930s, E. M. Forster wrote in 'What I Believe' the possibly ultimate statement of faith of the between-the-wars intellectuals, who saw in the governments of the world nothing much to choose between. By then a good many had become disillusioned by the failure of the Marxist hope in Soviet Russia, and felt if anything even more bleak about the prospects for democracy under capitalism. Forster's alternative was the doctrine of personal relations, already adumbrated in his novels many years before, most notably in *Howards End* and *A Passage to India* – in 1910 and 1924 respectively. But later in 'What I Believe' he made a number of remarkable observations on the theme, including the subsequently notorious assertion: 'If I had to choose between betraying my friend and betraying my country, I hope I should have the guts to betray my country' (66). Certain defenders of Burgess, Maclean, Philby, and Blunt recalled these words of Forster's; but those traitors betrayed their friends as well. Besides, he explicitly rejected the Soviet way, in the very essay from which the phrase comes. Greene provides a purer example of the truth of Forster's dictum, but no better refuge for the traitorousness of the Four. If it can be said that there is a plague on both the houses, Capitalism and Marxism equally, to betray one's country means nothing: friendship is everything; the choice is an easy one to make, and to make without regret. For Greene there is not the possibility of even a single cheer for democracy, but there remains the sense of loyalty to his friends. In *Ways of Escape* he says: 'I began *The Human Factor* more than ten years before it was published and abandoned it in despair after two or three years' work. . . . I abandoned it mainly because of the Philby affair [Philby and Greene were friends]. My double agent Maurice Castle bore no resemblance in character or motive to Philby . . . but I disliked the idea of the novel being taken for a *roman à clef* ' (298).

Greene's adeptness as a writer of thrillers comes into play in the final sections of *The Human Factor*. Greene has a most judicious talent for the juxtaposition of concrete detail (the Caribbean-style hotel at Heathrow, the partly-furnished apartment in Moscow) with revelation and withholding of information, and the intro-duction of unplanned encounters such as that of Castle with an acquaintance at the London airport hotel. But Greene makes the suspense aroused by his sure sense of what details to include and what to scamp fit neatly the sense of the novel as a whole; for instance, Halliday Senior's revelation of his Party membership and the reasons for having joined – these come as a surprise to Castle as they do also to the reader. Their inclusion makes possible the sketching out of the contrast between Castle and Halliday. For all the good sense, or the approximately good sense that the bookseller talks, Castle simply isn't a believer, not of this sort: 'If we drove for a century, Halliday [they are on their way to Heathrow together] you wouldn't convert me' (282). And when they part, Halliday gives Castle a copy of *The Way We Live Now*. But when he gets into the hotel room and tries to read the Trollope novel, Castle is baulked: 'he found it was not a book which could distract him from the way he lived now' (286). Unlike Sir John Hargreaves he cannot lose himself in the elaborate structures of society; for Castle such structures no longer exist except as mere shadows.

The ultimate turn of the screw is given by Boris in Moscow: 'Your people imagined they had an agent in place, here in Moscow. But it was we who had planted him on them. Your reports authenticated him in the eyes of your service, they could check them, and all the time he was passing them other information which we wanted them to believe. That was the real value of your reports. A nice piece of deception. But then came the Muller affair and Uncle Remus. We decided the best way to counter Uncle Remus was publicity – we couldn't do that and leave you in London. You had to be our source – you brought Muller's notes with you' (331).

The autumnal quality of *The Human Factor* – the action of which even begins in October – has more than one source. There is unquestionably the darkening imagination with its focus on the universal destruction that the hydrogen bomb, or bombs, can bring at the push of a button. It is an imagination with which all must live who dwell in this end of the twentieth century. From the viewpoint of Greene's work as a whole it may be said that this novel centres more explicitly than any of his other work on the sense of man-made apocalypse, a sense that has been intrinsic, though less specific, from the beginning. Greene's wanderlust having taken him to the parts of the world where the darkest possibilities of man's fate have been all too poignantly realized, the impulse to find in Mexico, in Haiti, in Africa, in Vietnam and elsewhere, the worst possible fears for mankind acted out; this has been the effort to map what has been called Greeneland. Obviously there is something entirely personal, entirely individual, about Greene's vision of mankind and of man's world. Neither was it necessary for him to go abroad in order to discover such bleakness; one of Greene's most disturbing locales is the Sussex sea coast of *Brighton Rock* (1938), well before the Manhattan Project. In *The Human Factor*, Castle has found that 'fear and love are indivisible' (119), but the sentiment runs throughout Greene's work.

Such is the life-long personal source of the sense of an ending that Greene's novel exhibits – never mind that after *The Human Factor* comes *Monsignor Quixote*, much more full of cheer, but hardly a work that could be called a comedy, comic though it is in its depiction of the wanderings of a present-day Quixote together with his Sancho, the Communist ex-mayor of the small town in which Quixote is the parish priest: for the good Quixote is old, and the novel ends with his death. In both these late novels, the central figure is an old man: Castle at sixty-two realizes that he will not live to see what he would normally have expected to be able to see and share in his family life – because Sarah is much younger than he, and Sam a young boy. Castle thinks of old age and death; lying in bed with Sarah, 'he wondered whether this was how the happiness of old age, which he had sometimes seen on a stranger's face, might come about, but he would be dead long before she reached old age. Old age was something they would never be able to share' (29).

The last words of *The Human Factor* do not signalize the end of an ordeal, but a commencement: the hope for the reunion of Sarah and Maurice appears to fade. On the telephone from England to

Moscow, Sarah says: ' "Maurice, Maurice, please go on hoping", but in the long unbroken silence which followed she realized that the line to Moscow was dead' (339). The shift from the vantage point of Castle to that of Sarah distances the reader from him enough to bring about the realization that he is not to have the last word, not the last thought. For him hope is gone; but for Sarah, there is, no doubt desperately, still a tie, or the hope of a tie; the last word, or rather the last silence, of the novel, speaks – the human factor. For Greene as for Conrad the human factor is love, but their novels will allow no-one to suppose that the love that is being sketched out in *The Secret Agent* and *The Human Factor* is a universal or a western or even a Christian kind of love. Their great skill, and great achievement, is to place love in our century, to show how and to what extent love is possible and impossible. Greene the Christian in all his work specifies with increasing pessimism the lineaments of the human factor, but the rootedness of love as dangerous enterprise is already signalled in the epigraph from Conrad: to love is not simply to run a risk but to face the certainty of the failure not of the enterprise itself, though that failure is entailed in the more general failure brought about by the reifying forces of the civilized structures that twentieth-century man lives within. 'A man in love walks through the world like an anarchist, carrying a time bomb' (178–79) – such is the reflection of Castle, summoning up a remembrance of the Professor at the end of *The Secret Agent*, that loveless creature who did not know the meaning of human attachment. Therefore the final note of Greene's novel, for all the fatality of the broken telephone line, sketches the sense of a future in which love will be, must be, renewed.

References

1. INTRODUCTION

Alter, Robert. *Motives for Fiction*. Cambridge, Mass.: Harvard UP, 1984.

Barthes, Roland. 'Historical Discourse'. In *Structuralism a Reader*, ed. Michael Lane, 145–55. London: Cape, 1970.

Bloomfield, Morton. 'Authenticating Realism and the Realism of Chaucer'. *Thought* 39 (1964) 335–58.

Booth, Wayne C. *The Rhetoric of Fiction*. 2nd ed. Chicago: Chicago UP, 1983.

Brown, Marshall. 'The Logic of Realism: A Hegelian Approach'. *PMLA* 96 (1981), 224–41.

Caserio, Robert. *Plot, Story, and the Novel*. Princeton: Princeton UP, 1979.

Derrida, Jacques. *Grammatology*. Trans. Gayatri Spivak. Baltimore: Johns Hopkins UP, 1974.

Foucault, Michel. *The Archaeology of Knowledge*. Trans. A. M. Sheridan Smith. New York: Harper & Row, 1972.

Gearhart, Suzanne. *The Open Boundary of History and Fiction: A Critical Approach to the French Enlightenment*. Princeton: Princeton UP, 1984.

Genette, Gérard. 'Boundaries of Narrative'. *New Literary History* 8 (1976), 1–13.

——. *Narrative Discourse*. Trans. Jane E. Lewin. Ithaca: Cornell UP, 1980.

Hamburger, Käte. *The Logic of Literature*. Trans. M. J. Rose. 2nd ed. Bloomington: Indiana UP, 1973.

Harman, Barbara Leah. 'The Fiction of Coherence: George Herbert's "The Collar" ', *PMLA* 93 (1978), 865–77.

James, Henry. Preface. *The Portrait of a Lady*. The Novels and Tales of Henry James 3. New York: Scribner, 1907.

Jameson, Fredric. *The Political Unconscious: Narrative as a Socially Symbolic Act*. London: Methuen, 1981.

Kermode, Frank. *Essays on Fiction 1971–82*. London: Routledge, 1983.

Lentricchia, Frank. *After the New Criticism*. Chicago: Chicago UP, 1980.

Lodge, David. 'Mimesis and Diegesis in Modern Fiction'. In Anthony Mortimer, ed., *Contemporary Approaches to Narrative.* SPELL: Swiss Papers in English Language and Literature (1984). Tübingen: Gunter Narr, 1984, 89–108.

Naipaul, V. S. *The Return of Eva Perón.* Harmondsworth: Penguin, 1981.

Ong, Walter J. *Interfaces of the Word: Studies in the Evolution of Consciousness and Culture.* Ithaca: Cornell UP, 1977.

Rimmon-Kenan, Shlomith. *Narrative Fiction: Contemporary Poetics.* London: Methuen, 1983.

Slatoff, Walter. *With Respect to Readers.* Ithaca: Cornell UP, 1977.

Todorov, Tzvetan. *The Poetics of Prose.* Trans. Richard Howard. Ithaca: Cornell UP, 1977.

Toliver, Harold. *Animate Illusions: Explorations of Narrative Structure.* Lincoln, Neb: U of Nebraska P, 1974.

Torgovnick, Marianna. *Closure in the Novel.* Princeton: Princeton UP, 1981.

Walcott, Derek. *Dream on Monkey Mountain and Other Plays.* New York: Farrar, Straus: 1970.

Watt, Ian. 'The Ironic Tradition in Augustan Prose from Swift to Johnson'. *Restoration and Augustan Prose.* Los Angeles: Clark Library, 1956. 19–46.

White, Hayden. *Metahistory: The Historical Imagination in Nineteenth-Century Europe.* Baltimore: Johns Hopkins UP, 1973.

——. *Tropics of Discourse: Essays in Cultural Criticism.* Baltimore: Johns Hopkins UP, 1978.

——. 'The Value of Narrativity in the Representation of Reality'. In W. J. T. Mitchell, ed., *On Narrative.* Chicago: Chicago UP, 1981. 1–23.

2.   CRUSOE THEN AND NOW

I   Robinson Crusoe: or, Do It Yourself

Alkon, Paul. *Defoe and Fictional Time.* Athens: U of Georgia P, 1979.

Boardman, Michael. *Defoe and the Uses of Narrative.* New Brunswick: Rutgers UP, 1983.

Defoe, Daniel. *Robinson Crusoe.* 1719. Ed. J. Donald Crowley. London: Oxford UP, 1972.

Genette, Gérard.*Narrative Discourse: An Essay in Method.* 1972. Trans. Jane E. Lewin. Ithaca: Cornell UP, 1980.

Hunter, J. Paul. *The Reluctant Pilgrim: Defoe's Emblematic Method and Quest for Form in 'Robinson Crusoe'.* Baltimore: Johns Hopkins UP, 1966.

Jameson, Fredric. 'Metacommentary', *PMLA* 86 (1971): 9–18.

Macheray, Pierre. *A Theory of Literary Production.* Trans. Geoffrey Wall. London: Routledge, 1978.

Novak, Maximillian E. *Defoe and the Nature of Man.* London: Oxford UP, 1963.

——. *Economics and the Fiction of Defoe.* Berkeley: U of California P, 1962.

——. *Realism, Myth, and History in Defoe's Fiction.* Lincoln, Neb.: U of Nebraska P, 1983.

Olney, James, ed. *Autobiography: Essays Theoretical and Critical.* Princeton: Princeton UP, 1980.

Pascal, Roy. *Design and Truth in Autobiography.* London, Routledge, 1960.

Richetti, John. *Defoe's Narratives.* London: Oxford UP, 1975.

Ross, Angus. Introduction. *Robinson Crusoe.* London: Penguin, 1965.

Sill, Geoffrey M. *Defoe and the Idea of Fiction 1713–1719.* Newark: U of Delaware P, 1983.

Starobinski, Jean. 'The Style of Autobiography'. In Olney: 73–83.

Starr, George A. *Defoe and Spiritual Autobiography.* Princeton: Princeton UP, 1965.

Sutherland, James, ed. *Robinson Crusoe and Other Writings.* Boston: Houghton, Mifflin, 1968.

Watt, Ian. *The Rise of the Novel.* Berkeley: U of California P, 1957.

White, Hayden. 'The Value of Narrativity in the Representation of Reality'. In W. J. T. Mitchell, ed., *On Narrative.* Chicago: Chicago UP, 1981. 1–23.

II   The Mosquito Coast: Isolation as Madness

Carpentier, Alejo. *Los Pasos perdidos.* México: Ibero-Americana, 1953. Translated into English as *The Lost Steps.* Trans. Harriet de Onis. London: Gollancz, 1956.

Sulzberger, C. L., et al. *The American Heritage Picture History of*

World War II 2. New York: American Heritage, 1966.

Theroux, Paul. *The Mosquito Coast*. London: Hamish Hamilton, 1981.

3. THE EMERGENT WOMAN

I   Emma: Perfection under Threat

Austen, Jane. *Emma*. 1816. The Novels of Jane Austen 4. Ed. R. W. Chapman. 3rd ed. Oxford: Clarendon, 1933.

——. *Letters to Her Sister Cassandra and Others*. Ed. R. W. Chapman. 2nd ed. London: Oxford UP, 1952.

Brownstein, Rachel. *Becoming a Heroine*. New York: Viking, 1982.

Butler, Marilyn. *Jane Austen and the War of Ideas*. Oxford: Clarendon, 1975.

Cecil, David. *Poets and Storytellers*. London: Constable, 1949. A reprint of the Leslie Stephen Lecture, published by the Cambridge UP in 1935.

Gillie, Christopher. *A Preface to Jane Austen*. London: Longman, 1974.

Miller, D. A. *Narrative and Its Discontents: Problems of Closure in the Traditional Novel*. Princeton: Princeton UP, 1981.

Roberts, Warren. *Jane Austen and the French Revolution*. London: Macmillan, 1979.

Schorer, Mark. 'Fiction and the Matrix of Analogy'. *Kenyon Review* 12 (1949). 539–560.

II   Howards End and the Denial of Doom

Bradbury, Malcolm. 'Howards End'. *Forster: A Collection of Critical Essays*. Ed. Malcolm Bradbury. Englewood Cliffs: Prentice, 1966. 128–43.

Forster, E. M. *Aspects of the Novel* (The Clark Lectures, 1927). Abinger Edition 12. Ed. Oliver Stallybrass. London: Arnold, 1974.

——. *Howards End*. 1910. Abinger Edition 4. Ed. Oliver Stallybrass. London: Arnold, 1973.

——. *Marianne Thornton*. New York: Harcourt, 1956.

——. 'The Raison d'Etre of Criticism in the Arts'. 1947. In *Two*

Cheers for Democracy. Abinger Edition 2. Ed. Oliver Stallybrass. London: Arnold, 1972, 105–18.

——. *Selected Letters* 1. Ed. Mary Lago and P. N. Furbank. Cambridge, Mass.: Harvard UP, 1983.

——. 'What I Believe'. 1938. In *Two Cheers*, 65–73.

Gillie, Christopher. *A Preface to Forster*. London: Longman, 1983.

Leavis, F. R. *The Common Pursuit*. London: Chatto, 1952.

Macaulay, Rose. *The Writings of E. M. Forster*. London: Hogarth, 1938.

McConkey, James. *The Novels of E. M. Forster*. Ithaca: Cornell UP, 1957.

Rosecrance, Barbara. *Forster's Narrative Vision*. Ithaca: Cornell UP, 1982.

Stone, Wilfred. *The Cave and the Mountain*. London: Oxford UP, 1966.

Trilling, Lionel. *E. M. Forster*. London: Hogarth, 1944.

4.   ANARCHY AND APOCALYPSE

I   The Secret Agent: The Beginning of the End

Batchelor, John. *The Edwardian Novelists*. London: Duckworth, 1982.

Beerbohm, Max. 'The Feast by J*s*ph C*nr*d'. *The Bodley Head Max Beerbohm*. Ed. David Cecil. London: Bodley Head, 1970. 351–54.

Conrad, Joseph. *Letters to R. B. Cunninghame Graham*. Ed. C. T. Watts. Cambridge: Cambridge UP, 1969.

——. *Works*. Uniform Edition. 22 vols. London: Dent, 1923–28. 'Autocracy and War' (1905) is reprinted in the volume entitled *Notes on Life and Letters* (1924), 83–114.

Cox, C. B. *Joseph Conrad: The Modern Imagination*. London: Dent, 1974.

Ensor, R. C. K. *England: 1870–1914*. Oxford: Clarendon, 1936.

Hay, Eloise Knapp. *The Political Novels of Joseph Conrad: A Critical Study*. Chicago: Chicago UP, 1963. Repr. 1981.

Karl, Frederick R. *Joseph Conrad: the Three Lives*. New York: Farrar, 1979.

Kermode, Frank. *Essays on Fiction, 1971–82*. London: Routledge, 1983.

Naipaul, V. S. 'Conrad's Darkness'. *The Return of Eva Perón.*

London: Penguin, 1981. 197–218.

Sherry, Norman. *Conrad's Western World*. Cambridge: Cambridge UP, 1971.

Watt, Ian. *Conrad in the Nineteenth Century*. Berkeley: U of California P, 1979.

Watt, Ian, ed. *Conrad: The Secret Agent: A Casebook*. London: Macmillan, 1973.

Woodcock, George. *Anarchism*. Cleveland: Meridian, 1962.

II The Human Factor and Hope Without Hope

Conrad, Joseph. *Victory: An Island Tale*. 1915. *Works*. Uniform Edition. 22 vols. London: Dent, 1923–28. *Victory* was published in this edition in 1923.

Forster, E. M. 'What I Believe'. 1938. *Two Cheers for Democracy*. Abinger Edition 2. Ed. Oliver Stallybrass. London: Arnold, 1972, 65–73.

Greene, Graham. *The Human Factor*. London: Bodley Head, 1978.

——. *Ways of Escape*. London: Bodley Head, 1980.

Spurling, John. *Graham Greene* (Contemporary Writers). London: Methuen, 1983.

Index

111